Stephanie Crumley-Effinger

DAVID AUGSBURGER

SUSTAINING LOVE

HEALING & GROWTH
In the Passages of Marriage

DAVID AUGSBURGER

SUSTAINING
LOVE

HEALING & GROWTH
In the Passages of Marriage

GL
Regal Books

A Division of GL Publications
Ventura, California, U.S.A.

Published by Regal Books
A Division of GL Publications
Ventura, California 93006
Printed in U.S.A.

Library of Congress Cataloging-in-Publication Data

Augsburger, David W.
    Sustaining love : healing and growth in the passages of marriage / by David
Augsburger.
            p.   cm.
    Bibliography: p.
    Includes index.
    ISBN 0-8307-1309-3
    1. Marriage—Religious aspects—Christianity. I. Title.
BV835.A94   1989
646.7'8—dc19   88-18656
                                                                         CIP

1 2 3 4 5 6 7 8 9 10/ 91 90 89 88

Rights for publishing this book in other languages are contracted by Gospel
Literature International (GLINT) foundation. GLINT also provides technical
help for the adaptation, translation, and publishing of Bible study resources
and books in scores of languages worldwide. For further information, contact
GLINT, Post Office Box 488, Rosemead, California, 91770, U.S.A., or the
publisher.

CONTENTS

FOREWORD

Sustaining Love is a recovery-of-hope book written to help couples rebuild hope when relationships feel hopeless, to renew hope in couples who have lost hope—hope in each other, hope in marriage, hope in their own ability to make something fulfilling out of a disintegrating marriage.

Within these pages lies hope for hurting marriages. And every marriage hurts at key points in its development. These critical points are times of turning—toward the better or the worse.

Its long view of marriage is the strength of this book. Not a quick fix for marital problems, it is a hopeful vision of marriage as a joint journey of many passages. It faces and maximizes on the "marriages within a marriage" which unfold in serial progression, decade by decade, and offers help in bridging the turbulent times that mark the passages from one marriage to the next.

Throughout *Sustaining Love*, David Augsburger affirms the hope that exists for troubled marriages. While no marriage is a stranger to some level of troubledness at key times of change and growth, there are also possibilities for hope at such stages. I am particularly interested in this theme, so winsomely presented in *Sustaining Love,* because of my work with the Recovery of Hope Network (see page 228 for more information about this ministry to troubled marriages).

Read on and discover how a long view of the marital journey can be freeing, even transforming.

Explore the marriages within your marriage.

Stephen K. Wilke, Ph.D.
President,
Recovery of Hope Network, Inc.
Wichita, Kansas

1
TRANSFORMATIONS

TRANSFORMATIONS:

MARRIAGES WITHIN A MARRIAGE

I love you.
I must be with you.
I'll never leave you.
You'll always be first.
We are in love.

I still like you, but
I can't go on without change.
I need space, I need respect.
I need to be me as well as "we".
We are in struggle.

I find you surprising.
What I liked at the first
I came to resent in you.
Now I wouldn't change it at all.
We are learning love.

When I'm with you
I feel at home, complete.
When we're apart
I am at peace, secure.
We are loved.

Year One

She: "We can't find enough time to do all the things together that we enjoy. Sure, we've had our little tiffs, but nothing that really threatened our closeness. When he's away, I feel like a part of me is missing."

He: "I can't wait until my work is finished in the evenings and we can get on with doing our thing. We both enjoy so many things that excites the other, she's such fun to be with."

Year Ten

She: "I think we have as much closeness as most, it's just that, well, the kids need their time, my job is pretty demanding, and he expects so much from me for the little he gives. If I'm going to have room to be me, I've got to fight for it."

He: "I don't know, there's not much to say. We're both busy with our careers and the family. There's not the fire in our loving that we started out with. She talks more about equality than about being close. I get pretty tired of her pushing me either her way or away."

Year Twenty

She: "I learned to really like the guy, somewhere along the way. We had about five empty years, then three bad ones when it wasn't sure that we'd make it. Then we turned a corner. Somewhere. And somehow, it was like a different, a new marriage."

He: "I guess we're survivors. A lot of our friends' marriages broke up a few years back. We almost did too. Except, things changed somehow. The stuff that bugged the dickens out of me didn't seem so important anymore. Maybe it's what I liked about her to begin with. We're comfortable, and good . . . yeah, good together."

Year Thirty

She: "I really like that man. Now we've got time to plan things, to go places, to play together. The kids are more like friends, like fellow adults. And the two of us? There's a kind of depth, a deep safety and a freedom we didn't have before."

He: "I said to her the other day, 'If I'd known how to feel and to talk about my feelings when we started out, we could have avoided some of those rough times. But they were good, too, in their own way. Now we understand, we really know each other."

Four marriages, as a minimum, occur as couples mature through the four central decades of change:

The Dream of the 20s
The Disillusionment of the 30s
The Discovery of the 40s
The Depth of the 50s.

This listing is one way of describing the sequence of marriages within a marriage that makes up a growing relationship. There are many styles of being a couple, and a variety of ways to define the stages we go through in achieving adulthood together.

We shall use a variety of perspectives, a whole spectrum of language shades and tints to explore the serial monogamy which unfolds in the struggle between closeness and distance, dependency and individualism, absorption and abandonment, lovemaking and fighting that all contribute to a man and a woman creating a common life together.

"Serial monogamy" with the same partner is the desirable process, although for half the North American population the sequence is broken off with one partner and started over with a second or a third. Failure to negotiate the passages between "the marriages within a marriage" makes divorce more likely and complicates immensely the normal patterns of growth. It is the treacherous passage into and out of the second marriage which sinks many basically good relationships that might have matured and become deeply satisfying and fulfilling alliances.

"Serial polygamy (polyandry)" with the same partner is a more accurate description than "serial monogamy," since not only the marriage undergoes transformation; the persons change too. Given the freedom to grow, partners make major shifts in values, commitments, life-styles, priorities, conflict styles, and degrees of expressing feelings and experiencing intimacy.

We may be now entering our fourth marriage to each other—the same partners—yet the marriages are between significantly different persons. The two nice, compliant, concealed romantics of the first marriage would be quite uncomfortable with the candid confrontive realists that emerged in the second marriage or skeptical about the open mutual intimates of the third marriage. The changes in personality set both of us free from old patterns that created pain within us, the changes in marriage allowed us to set each other free from pain between us.

As persons change, the marriage changes. As the marriage is renegotiated, the persons grow. Each becomes more of what she always was, yet never has been; more of what he wanted to be, yet never could be.

In one's first marriage, inevitably, past experiences are blended with present excitement. The strengths and weaknesses of one's family of origin are woven into the hopes, dreams and goals that knit the two together. Each person maps the past onto the future, projects the family experienced in childhood and youth onto the partner and the partnership. This first marriage may be a joint creation of the two, but more frequently it is a merger of two pasts, a collision of two powerful family forces that hold together from 7 to 10 years with the miracle glue of denial and avoidance—denial of what is pushing in from the past and avoidance of what is pulling them toward a different future.

As the first marriage begins to come apart, anxiety rises and the desperation only adds more glue. We'll stick together—for appearances, for the kids, for religious reasons, for safety against the unknown. But the glue will not hold. The denial breaks. A new marriage may be emerging out of the unknown and unexamined.

If the couple survives the explorations of the second marriage with its testing and probing, with its acting out and working through, then a third marriage may break upon them. Reaching the third level is like breaking through to new respect for each other's identity, new discoveries about both distance and closeness, about intimacy and autonomy. Now free to be both near and far the couple can begin working toward a fourth marriage of depth and a sense of destiny.

Courage to Grow

This joint journey requires a lot of personal as well as marital growth. Such growth entails four revisions of self-understanding; four kinds of self-esteem, four stages of handling differences and difficulties. Included is a lot of *letting go* of old habits that don't work any longer, a good deal of *letting be* on issues that one comes to realize are not all that important, and a surprising amount of *letting come* what will as the new relationship unfolds. The experience of oneself, of one's partner and of the relationship that connects us is so different that one looks back with surprise that we stayed so long in that old way of being. One looks at the other with wider eyes, seeing new sides, feeling new feelings, understanding new insights about this well-accustomed yet provocatively unfamiliar person.

Life and growth should be redundant words, but observation of others and reflection on oneself reveals embarrassing periods of being stuck in routine. Growth and marriage should also be repetitive, but most marriages alternate quiet periods of stability with brief passages of change and maturation. Growth and change are not ends in themselves. In fact, growth for growth's sake is the philosophy of a cancer cell. The goal of growth is wholeness, completeness, maturity. The real failure in life is to fail to grow toward such goals; sin is, among other things, the refusal to grow.

Your present marriage is only one of many you will experience if you continue life together. Marriage is not a single style of relating, committing, trusting, negotiating, conflicting and growing. When there is growth—and marriage is the basic means for growth in our society—then there will be multiple marriages, serial marriages, a series of marriages that unfold as the persons grow.

I should say the relation
between any two
decently married people
changes profoundly
every few years,
often without their knowing
anything about it;
though every change causes pain,
even if it brings a certain joy.
The long course of marriage
is a long event
of perpetual change,
in which a man and woman
mutually build up their souls
and make themselves whole.
It is like rivers flowing on,
through new country,
always unknown.[1]

Marriage has become the primary vehicle for personal growth in Western society. It offers one of the few safe arenas in which a person can discard the illusions, fantasies and false hopes of childhood and grow toward authentic adulthood. In the permanence of a marriage relationship one can develop the qualities of adulthood that can be simulated or bypassed in other relationships—qualities such as honesty, self-disclosing, humility, tolerance for and love of differences. This deeper growth rarely happens without the struggle of living intimately with a marriage partner; such growth isn't achieved in isolation.

"Marriage," says family therapist Carl Whitaker, "is the central focus for enlightenment and the natural therapeutic process in the culture. Marriage is the greatest ordeal in life."[2]

More than any previous society, we place exorbitant demands on marriage. In earlier ages, marriage was expected to be an economically productive, biologically procreative and socially permanent bonding of families. In modern Western society, the expectations of marriage include companionship, emotional fulfillment, mutual growth in personal identity and progressive levels of intimacy.

For centuries, marriage was not a relationship requiring examination and renegotiation. Marriage was a given against which one adjusted the other relationships and responsibilities of life. "An unexamined life is not worth living," Socrates observed. He also said, "Call no man unhappy until he is married." What Xantippe said is not recorded. The unexamined marriage was taken as the inevitable process of fulfilling the roles and routines of being male, female, marital and parental. In an age of inflated expectations, many marriages still unfold without intentional reflection, readjustment and review. And some unexamined marriages, like an unexamined life, may seem to drift through time without crisis or change, but in reality such marriages have locked into their first understanding and refused to keep pace with the changes in either the person's own maturation or the evolution of the family situation.

Taking a Long View of Marriage

A commitment to permanence in marriage is necessary for real creativity. Only when one takes a long view of marriage is one truly free to risk the exploration of both the highs and the lows, the peaks and the valleys of a growing relationship. When marriage is seen as a joint journey of mutual growth, a developmental process over a long period of time then difficult periods can be put into perspective.

Couples in shock often sit in angry irritable depression or in silent exhausted withdrawal when they come for their first session of marital therapy:

"We've had a reasonable good relationship until the last two years, then it began to turn sour," she reports.

"I don't want to go on this way," he says, "but I can't see cashing in after seven years of marriage."

We sketch a time line of their marriage, look at the stress points and the celebrations. Then alongside we draw the normal pattern of original romantic closeness, the beginnings of the first marriage breaking down, the threat of the two breaking up, the possibilities of breaking through to second and third marriages and the ambiance of the room begins to brighten. For the first time, perhaps, they are taking a long view of relationship, a developmental perspective that allows them to see the present checkmate not as a stalemate that must end in divorce, but as an end of one game and the beginning of another with the same players. Changing players would rarely do more than repeat the same game with a different opponent. But starting over with the same partner allows for true creativity.

Creative change in marriage is facilitated by an understanding—a long view—of the four basic "marriages within a marriage."

Each of these four marriages has different ways of handling goals, differences, conflict, feelings, intimacy, communication, roles and life meaning. We will explore the sequence of stages that typically occur in these areas.

Obviously, since no two people are alike, it follows that no marriages are identical either. Therefore, many developmental models of stages in marriage are forced to be superficial. The model may include stages such as honeymoon, career search, parenting, empty nest, retirement marriage. In order to include all marriages the model is forced to exclude the deeper dynamics and major in commonalities.

If one risks looking for deeper patterns, as we will do in this map of marriage, then one must construct models that explain the deep tensions between union and separation, between growing in couplehood and growth in personhood. Such model building runs the risk that one stage will be exaggerated for some and much less marked for others. Couples who came from families which denied differences and avoided conflict are more likely to exaggerate the conflicts of the early stages of marriage or try to continue the first marriage lifelong. In contrast, persons from more open expressive families may move into mutually satisfying ways of resolving conflict in early marriage and have a less dramatic second stage.

However, the patterns of four basic marriages which are sketched in the following chapters are grounded in wide marital research and clinical observation. They do recur with high frequency, with a surprising regularity. The story of any one of us is, in some measure, the story of us all.

"There are only two or three human stories and they go on repeating themselves fiercely as if they had never happened before" wrote Willa Cather, the brilliant American author.[3] Our marital stories do have a striking similarity, once one gets beneath individual differences of historical detail.

Variation Is a Sign of Health

Where your experience differs from the stages of marriage outlined here, congratulate yourself. The more difficulty and pain in marriages, the more similar are their patterns; the more healthy and free the persons, the more variety and creativity emerges in the relationships. Each time you find that a suggested pattern does not fit, celebrate the health and freedom that you have inherited from your family past or chosen in your family present.

"Happy families are all alike. Every unhappy family is unhappy in its own way," wrote Leo Tolstoy as the opening line of *Anna Karenina*. Those two short sentences are a marvelously precise description of his novel which explores the uniqueness of one unhappy marriage, but the book has become a great classic of literature because it is an unhappy family so similar in its unhappiness to the unhappiness that happens in all families.

Yet the truth is the exact opposite of Tolstoy's assertion. Happy families exist in many forms, many types, many kinds. They grow in a variety of directions which are remarkably different. They allow for a much wider latitude in development of the marriage, of individuation of the partners, of differentiation of the children than do less happy families.

Unhappy families are more similar in their rigidity, their repetition of painful patterns of behavior, their stereotypic roles and relationships. They are often locked into one of a relatively limited number of life plots—what Cather called "the two or three human stories that go on repeating themselves fiercely as if they had never happened before." These basic plots or stories are often constructed around a shared need to not acknowledge an underground secret, not face an old pattern of hurting each other, not examine an old family myth, not grieve for a tragedy, not forgive and forget a transgression. So they get repeated again and again, and again.

I wish my life, my marriage, my growth had been less repetitious, less locked into the basic plots of human folly and weakness, but it is not so. However, the future is still unwritten. The next chapters of the story are open ended. To accept the death of one stage and to be reborn into the next is not easy.

Happy families make room for each other's growth by taking a long view of change. Change is always a threat at the moment of choice and action, but a long view allows us to trust each other in the process of growth. The usual, even inevitable human response is to say, (1) "Don't change." This is followed by the command, (2) "Change back." When this is not obeyed, it is supported by the threat, (3) "Obey, or else . . . or else you will suffer . . . or else God will get you . . . or else you will fail and the sky will fall." If this does not end the process of change, a period of (4) grudging respect will slowly emerge. Then eventually the other persons will say, (5) "Why did it take you so long to make such an obvious decision. We knew it was right all along." These five responses are as regular and natural as phototropism—as a plant turning toward the sun.[4]

Knowing about the stages of resistance to change does not end them, it only shortens them. Each of us continues to be threatened by another's movement when it challenges our basic expectations and assumptions. I have known about this resistance dance for years, have both suffered and later smiled when it happened with my own parents and siblings. Yet I do all five automatically when my wife or daughters make a significant movement in a surprising way.

Taking a long view of growth, change and maturation helps us shorten our resistance, and at times even to welcome each other's transitions from one life stage to another. The more open we are to variety, individuality and novelty in family relationships, the healthier the family structure and the family members. In contrast, the family which creates carbon-copy patterns of conformity violates something very precious and essential to our humanness—the distinct integrity of each person. Accepting another person as she is, as he is, is also accepting his right to grow, her right to become.

An Overview of the Journey

The marriages within a marriage can be examined from many perspectives. Each stage has a complexity, a richness, a multidimensional character that defies simple definition or description.

In the following chapters we will explore these stages

by tracing significant themes. Some of the central themes are: which goals, what kind of communication, what sort of conflict over differences and similarities, what style of intimacy, which roles, what meaning and what hope characterize the marriage. In the table of stages these themes are outlined for an overview of the four marriages that unfold. All things being equal—which they never are—these stages correspond to the 20s, 30s, 40s, 50s. But the first may be lengthened for 20 years or turned into a more permanent life-style—such as it is.

Or couples may separate as the first stage is coming apart, then lock into it desperately with a second partner. If they have grown and gained much from the first marriage, the stages may be more brief the second time around. So as varied as these stages are from couple to couple, the themes are worth pursuing through the stages and the passages which connect and transform them.

If you find your marriage stuck in a stage—as we all have been and will be again—then these thematic descriptions of the maturing journey of marriage may help you break loose.

If you find the old marriage dying, and hope is draining away, then this vision of marriage with a longer trajectory may reawaken hope that it can be recreated. Ending a marriage when only a stage of marriage needs to die is an unfortunate choice, in many cases. Far better to reinvent the relationship and rediscover love.

The late Sidney Jourard wrote these provocative words in his classic book *The Transparent Self*.

> I have encouraged spouses who find themselves in a dead marriage, but who still find it meaningful to try to live together, *to begin a series of experiments in their ways of relating.*

FOUR MARRIAGES WITHIN A MARRIAGE

	MARRIAGE ONE	MARRIAGE TWO	MARRIAGE THREE	MARRIAGE FOUR
GOALS	DREAM We marry to fulfill the Dream—personal, marital, career and communal dreams.	DISILLUSIONMENT The Dream fails us. Or we sacrifice the marital to gain the career and so on.	DISCOVERY We discover reality beyond the Dream, we discover each other.	DEPTH We develop depth in our selves, our marriage, our life together.
COMMUNICATION	EXPECTATION We communicate out of expectations of what is meant, needed, wanted, obligated, necessary.	MANIPULATION We manipulate by persuading, seducing, coercing, evading and avoiding to get what we want.	INVITATION We discover that true communication is invitation and work toward equality.	DIALOGUE We develop dialogue with genuine mutuality and equality in our communication.
FEELINGS	EXCUSE We are afraid of, embarrassed by, cautious with, concealed about or unaware of feelings.	EXPLODE We risk sharing feelings, but find them painfully threatening, often uncontrolled, unfocused, confused and confusing.	EXPRESS We own and express feelings with freedom and with both candor and caring.	EXPERIENCE We flow with both our feelings and thoughts.
DIFFERENCES	ACCOMMODATE We tolerate, accommodate, overlook differences to avoid conflict and obey the Dream.	ELIMINATE We seek eo eliminate the objectionable differences in the partner by demanding change.	APPRECIATE We discover the differences are creative, necessary parts of each of us and of our marriage.	CELEBRATE We delight in our differences and develop them in each other.

CONFLICT	**AVOID** We avoid conflict as disruptive and destructive of the Dream.	**ATTACK** We explode with frustrated feelings, seek to eliminate differences through fighting, bargaining, pressuring.	**ADJUST** We discover more fair ways of fighting; we seek mutually satisfactory solutions more quickly.	**ACCEPT** We accept conflict as a healthy process and utilize it to work for mutual growth.
INTIMACY	**DEPENDENT** Intimacy is dependent on romance, on the moment, on the other's responses, on his/her "acting as prescribed."	**INDEPENDENT** Intimacy is touch and go, intense when things are going well, absent when there is tension or threat.	**INTERDEPENDENT** Intimacy now becomes truly possible as autonomy is balanced with solidarity.	**INTIMATE** Intimacy now develops freely in emotional, mental, social and spiritual levels.
ROLES	**COMPLEMENTARY** Relationships are shaped by complementary "fitting" of partner's strengths and weaknesses.	**SYMMETRICAL** Relationships are competitive, adversary, tit-for-tat struggles to claim personal identity	**PARALLEL** Relationships achieve balance, equal freedom and responsibility. Autonomy and intimacy are protected.	**INTERTWINED** Relationships are mutual, with both partners secure and satisfied whether near or far.
MEANING	**HOPES** Hope shaped by the Dream are largely false hopes which must eventually die for love to become truly alive.	**HOPELESSNESS** Hopes fade, falter and fail us. Life together becomes empty and alienated.	**HOPEFUL** Hope rises as we find that beneath the old hopes there is deeper, richer meaning to our life together.	**HOPE** True hope has emerged and pushes us onward from healing in the past, pulls us forward with the promise of the future.

People
do not
marry
people,
not real ones,
anyway:
They marry
what they think
the person is;
they marry illusions and images.

Many end their marriages
because the spouse
does not match
the internal image.[5]

The image or metaphor that underlies this experimentation is the view of serial polygamy to the same person . . . when one partner or the other finds continuation in the old way intolerable, the marriage in its legal form is usually dissolved . . . . It is also possible that the couple may struggle with the impasse and evolve a new marriage with each other.[6]

This book offers a series of experiments in seeing marriage with new eyes, seeing each other with new understanding and seeing life together as a new possibility.

Recovering the Freedom to Grow

The amount of growth possible in a marriage depends not only on the growth-space each person claims and each partner gives to the other, it depends also on the room to grow granted by the culture, community and faith group that surrounds the marriage.

Cultural patterns, after a generation or two, accumulate authority, then become absolutized as final and necessary. We sacralize what is flawed and fallible, we view as eternal what is only temporary, we narrow our options, we reduce our possibilities for growth. The prescriptions for marriage become constrictive, the patterns open to couples restricted to the basic complementary relationship.

A culturally prescribed marital pattern, such as male dominance/female submission, that has been assumed for generations comes to be seen not as a human compromise but as a divine commandment. We then read our cultural practices back into the Bible to find a single divinely authorized model for marriage. The Bible possesses many models for marriage and multiple patterns for male-female relationships spread out over a thousand years of history and drawn from a dozen cultures—Mesopotamian, Egyptian, Palestinian, Philistine, Moabite, Babylonian, Persian, Judean, Galilean, Roman, Greek to begin the list. This provides a rich field of models for Christian peoples of multiple cultures across many centuries.

But in every culture, people select the model and quote the texts which reinforce the ideal patterns of their particular community. The assumption that the man is to be the leader, the woman a follower and the marriage complementary which arises from the culture is then credited to biblical authority. We have a long tradition of transposing our own culture and its practices into the vastly different biblical context and then receiving them back again unchanged but endowed with divine authority.

The Bible does not offer us a marriage manual; in fact, it offers only occasional references to marriage and its meaning. No prophet or apostle gives us a systematic discussion of marriage. Jesus made only incidental remarks, except for a brief discussion in response to the question of justifiable divorce (Matt. 19:3-12; Mark 10:2-12). Basing His answer on Genesis 1:27; 2:24; 5:2, He teaches that the two become one, that the bond should not be broken and that these are the Creator's intentions. The shape of this marriage unity, the patterns of the husband-wife relationship are not a part of Jesus' teaching.

Apparently, He accepted the patterns of the Jewish culture which had nourished Him. When asked about levirate marriage—the obligation of a brother to conceive children with a widowed sister-in-law to continue his brother's name—Jesus tacitly accepts the practice (Mark 12:24-27). The consistent thread throughout all His comments on marriage is the call to consistent faithfulness, constant love and trustful hope. Jesus does not address the definition of the renewal of marriage practices.

The New Testament letters offer several brief references to marriage (1 Cor. 7:1, Eph. 5:22-33, Col. 3:18-19, Titus 2:4-5, 1 Pet. 3:1-7), but they do not give an outline of marriage patterns, the roles of the spouses, the normative style of relationships. Peter counsels submission by the wife, Paul recommends mutual submission, Luke (Acts 18:26) records the mutual equal relationship of Priscilla and Acquilla. Some leaders were single and recommended singleness as superior to marriage. Others were married, but offer us no information on how their faith shaped their union. Still others modeled joint sharing of service and witness.

We find more than one model for marriage relationships in the New Testament. The writings of Paul offer several models which apply Christian ethics to various cultural settings, and he shows no need to harmonize them or to force them into one model for all persons, all situations and certainly not for all time. The hierarchical model of 1 Corinthians 11 includes a strong teaching on interdependency in the same passage. The Ephesians 5:22-33 model calls for a reframing of the old hierarchical model into a mutually submissive relationship which moves toward equality by demanding radical sacrifice by males to revolutionize the status quo.

The recognition of gifts in both women and men in ministry, prophesy, leadership, teaching and service indicates the trajectory of transforming relationships in the New Testament community in which—in Christ—is neither male nor female. Just as there are no longer ethnic hierarchies, nor slave-and-master hierarchies, so also sexual hierarchies have come to an end in Christ (Gal. 3:28).

Not only does the Bible offer a wide range of models for relationship, it gives accurate incisive portrayals of humans at the best and worst in covenant-keeping and covenant-breaking. In Scripture, is a clear progression from seeing women as possessions, to persons, to full equals. Parallel trajectories in other areas of human relations are equally clear: from tribal views of personality in which the whole family is destroyed for the sin of one member to the full understanding of individual responsibility; from owner-slave economies to a community of equal, free and mutually interdependent disciples; from parents who possess life-and-death power over children who must give absolute obedience to parents and children who are to work out loving relationships modeled after the life-style of Jesus the Christ.

We accept these trajectories in the social and political realms and we must allow ourselves to experience the full transformation in marital and parental relationships; we cannot justify chain-of-command patterns in male-female or parent-child interaction by picking and choosing biblical quotations. There are cultural settings such as many Asian family patterns in which more vertical relationships are the norm. In these, families must struggle to find ways to be faithful to the way of Jesus while being congruent with their own cultural values. In Western families, the exaggeratedly horizontal patterns which are emerging from our culture of rugged individualism are an equally difficult context for working out Christian faithfulness.

Faith, Hope, Love and Justice

The Bible does not offer us detailed models for marriage relationships, but it offers us something far more applicable across the centuries, across cultural boundaries, across different family traditions. It offers revolutionary principles for organizing our lives, for reconstructing failing relationships and for confronting the injustices of our culture prophetically.

These central principles for constructive relationships emerge from the basic experience of faith, hope, love and justice:

Faith is the commitment to creative fidelity; it is faithfulness to each other before God. Faith is both a way of perceiving and of acting; it is believing and doing.

Hope is the call of creative trust; it is hopefulness with each other before God. Hope is both a push from within the "hopeful" hoper and the pull from the possibilities of the future.

Love is the choice to see the other partner as equally precious; it is loving-kindness that acts in equal regard. Love is a way of seeing, feeling, thinking and acting toward another.

Justice is the commitment to work out mutually satisfactory and visibly equitable sharing of opportunities, resources and responsibilities in living with others; it is a creative drive for fairness in all covenantal relationships. Justice goes beyond retribution for injuries, and redistribution of resources to a redemptive and releasing discovery of what is truly right, good and beautiful.

All four of these virtues—virtue meaning "spiritual power"—are the central energies of any enduring relationship. They provide the room to grow, the power to grow, the direction for creative growth.

As marriage relationships change throughout life—as any living relationship must—these key elements direct and shape the forms it takes. Keeping faith with each

THE MARITAL LIFE CYCLE

STAGE 1 18-21	STAGE 2 22-28	STAGE 3 29-31	STAGE 4 32-39	STAGE 5 40-42	STAGE 6 43-59	STAGE 7 60-
INITIAL COMMITMENT	PROVISIONAL COMMITMENT	CRISIS OF COMMITMENT	JOINT PRODUCTIVITY	SUMMING UP LIFE DIRECTION	EMBRACING LIFE WORK	CELEBRATING INTEGRITY
Shift from family of origin to new loyalty to each other.	Conscious levels of covenant are clarified and the other's response is integrated.	Conscious that unverbalized levels of contract are asserted. The unconscious levels emerge.	Covenanting deepens as life tasks of generativity: children, work, friends, service community-building.	Life trajectory receives mid-course review and evaluation. Future goals are sought.	Resolving conflicts and stabilizing marriage for the years of major contribution.	Achieving personal integrity with a sense of wisdom, gratitude, and mature prizing of live, of community and humanity.
Conflict: Original ties conflict with formation of new contract.	Conflict: Uncertainty about choice of partner, stress over choice of or decisions in parenting.	Conflict: Identity is being lost in intimacy, autonomy lost in solidarity. Union is separation, absorption vs. abandonment, power vs. powerlessness. Conflicts follow.	Conflict: Contrasting ways of achieving productivity, scheduling work, rearing children, setting priorities, relating to community.	Conflict: Partners perceive "success" differently, struggle over values, priorities, schedules and time usage.	Conflict: Differing rates, directions, depths of emotional and spiritual growth. Males become affiliative, females become assertive.	Conflict: Despair, stagnation, loss of vision, seizing of power in an unwillingness to trust the next generations.
Identity is still in formation while intimacy is being attempted.	Identity is becoming clear on positive issues.					

Marriage is a crisis	Parenting is a crisis	Maturing is a crisis	Productivity is a crisis	Mid-life crisis	Life development	Integrity crisis
(1) of separation from family of origin, (2) of definition of a self-identity, (3) of coalition with another self in intimacy.	(1) of generational imperative to continue dynasty, (2) of resolution of intimacy deficiencies by becoming a triad, (3) of identity clarification as an adult.	(1) of identity being asserted, (2) of intimacy being affirmed, (3) without the loss of either.	(1) of performance—identity usurping personhood, (2) of productivity absorbing energy, (3) of "success" drives draining off involvement in marriage, family, community.	(1) of individual fulfillment, reaching of personal dreams, achieving of goals; (2) of joint fulfillment, of sharing goals, of adjusting, sacrificing, reshaping dreams.	(1) concerns for life-fulfillment in inclusive ways; (2) integrations of maturing love, freeing children, accepting age; (3) fears of losing youth, health, dreams of unlived life.	(1) to embrace living and having lived with a profound joy and humble wisdom; (2) to see aging, life and death as gifts of the Creator to be accepted in grace.
Young Married Couple	Child-bearing Stage	Preschool Stage	School-age Stage	Teenage Stage	Launching Years (Empty Nest)	Middle Age / Post retirement

other through the changes of our lives results in a faithfulness that refuses to fold when the going gets rough, just as steadfast love continues to prize the other regardless of conflicts and contradictions.

If we were to assume that there is only one basic model which is biblically mandated, traditionally practiced and socially acceptable in the Christian community, then the room to grow could be limited to doing what we must do in better form or with greater diligence. Many Christian communities have attempted to prescribe exactly that—one marital pattern, one set of acceptable roles, one way for husbands and wives to relate to each other. This did violence, not only to the great variety in personalities from couple to couple, but to the differences within a marriage from stage to stage.

Christians who seek to be faithful to the whole of the Bible—the whole sweep of its message and movement—recognize that we do not find a prescribed pattern for all marriages; we do find all the essential resources for discussing and discerning how to live out wholesome and healthful marriages according to God's intentions for loving, faithful, hopeful, just relationships.

As Diana and David Garland conclude, this will of God does not homogenize all human relationships, but creatively reharmonizes them in every age, stage, culture.

> The message of scripture is timely as well as timeless, but its meaning for persons has different emphases and import in their context than it has for others in different times or places. As we determine what that message is, it must then be applied to our own ways of living together, in our own culture. An understanding of what marriage for Christians is must be

addressed from within the experience of Christians in each age and culture.[7]

Throughout marriage, each partner must be open to the growth, sensitive to the needs, committed to the welfare of the other person, as well as to oneself. So each continues to ask:

How can I love the partner that God has given me with a truly equal regard?

How shall I work out creative fidelity with the person God has entrusted me to with a genuine faithfulness?

How will I both offer and claim fairness and equity with the mate I have chosen before God and guarantee authentic justice?

How do I rediscover hope in moments of confusion and conflict to let our lives be shaped and reshaped by the God of Hope?

If separation should be chosen by my partner, how can I act in loving ways and respond in respect for the other's right to decide, even when I disagree with the choices being made?

EXERCISE 1:
THE MARRIAGE LIFE CYCLE _____

Instructions. There are many different maps of the stages of marriage. The following map is an integrative summary of the life stages, the conflicts peculiar to each, the crises that emerge stage by stage.

1. Look at the seven stages listed across the top. Discuss where you are now.
2. Review the stages you have already experienced. Have you finished the work in what preceded, are you

able to work on your present agenda without being flooded by the past?

3. Examine the next stage. Are you almost ready to enter it? Can you anticipate its difficulties? Do you yearn for its freedoms?

4. Look at the sequence of conflicts in the second row of paragraphs defining each stage's central conflicts. Discuss how you are working through the central conflict of this period.

5. Look at the final series of paragraphs defining the successive crises of marriage. Explore how you have handled the crises which are past. How are you working through the crisis which is with you now?

6. Now look look at the whole trajectory of the marital life cycle. How will you survive its crises? Can you pledge to turn them into opportunities for growth?

7. If your partner chooses to separate, how can you act redemptively even while coping with the pain of being rejected, while feeling anger at choices being made for you, and while struggling to discover what is your own part in the failing marriage?

8. If there is no recovery of hope for the marriage, can you accept the losses; gain what is useful from the pain; claim what is available in your self, your faith, your network of relationships—and continue to embrace life?

2

DIFFERENCES

DIFFERENCES:

ACCOMMODATE	ELIMINATE	APPRECIATE	CELEBRATE
We tolerate, accommodate, overlook, deny differences to avoid conflict and obey the Dream.	We try to eliminate differences in the other by demanding, pressuring, manipulating change.	We discover differences are necessary, indispensable, essential to personhood and to the marriage.	We delight in our differences. We welcome and develop them in each other and ourselves.

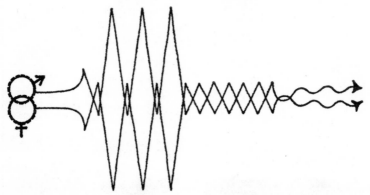

AVOID CONFLICT	ATTACK IN CONFLICT	ADJUST TO CONFLICT	ACCEPT CONFLICT
Deny that it is disruptive and destructive.	Accuse, excuse, attack, defend.	Adapt old dreams, adopt new behavior.	Welcome conflict by utilizing it for growth.

LISA   VS.   LARRY

"I don't know this man. I once thought I did, but then we agreed on at least a few things.

"After nine years together, I feel completely misunderstood whenever we try to talk, and I can't imagine why he feels the way he does about me.

"How could a marriage with such high hopes become so empty? We dated two years, we thought we had everything in common. We married with both families' blessing.

"We each had good jobs and liked our work. Sure it was a demanding schedule, but we had time for ski trips in the winter and camping in the summer.

"The time off from work for three years when Joey and Jan were little was frustrating for me. Larry was traveling a lot and not very available. When I went back to work, we both buried ourselves in our jobs and when we talked it was all about the kids.

"We didn't have much conflict until last year. Now he says it's day, I say it's night. He says it's winter I say it's summer. We don't see eye to eye on any thing. When things go wrong we can get into blaming each other for days.

"He's become a stranger to me."

"Our problems are all in Lisa's mind. She's got this idea that I don't love her anymore just because we often disagree, but that's the way life is. So what?

"My father and mother never agreed on anything. They stayed together for 63 years. So I don't see what all the fuss is about. We get along pretty well, compared to them.

"Lisa complains about my work schedule, but I think it's better if we're not in each other's hair so much. A couple has to adjust if they want to get ahead in life. My work really keeps me running, but it pays well.

"She criticizes my travel schedule, but she's away at her job every day too.

"She says I put my job ahead of the family, but that's not true since I'm doing it all for the family.

"She gripes about my golf, but I have to get exercise. And besides, it's usually with clients that I need to entertain, so it's part of my work.

"If she'd just lay off, we wouldn't have any real problems. I feel like this is a different marriage than we've had all through the years. She's like a different person the last year. Now that our youngest is in school you'd think there'd be less to worry about."

The first marriage of accommodating has ended. The second marriage of seeking to eliminate differences and attacking has begun.

We marry for our similarities.
We stay together for our differences.
Similarities satiate, differences attract.
Differences are rarely the cause of conflict in
marriage.
The problems arise from our similarities.
Differences are the occasion, similarities are
the cause.

The differences may serve as the triggering event, as
the issue for debate or the beef for our hassle, but it's the
similarities that create the conflict between us.

The very same differences that initially drew us
together, later press us apart and still later may draw us
near again. Differences first attract, then irritate, then
frustrate, then illuminate and finally may unite us. Those
traits that intrigue in courtship, amuse in early marriage
begin to chafe in time and infuriate in the conflicts of middle marriage; but maturation begins to change their meaning and the uniqueness of the other person becomes
prized, even in the very differences that were primary irritants.

It's not *that* we differ, but *how* we go about differing
that makes the difference between happiness and unhappiness. When we differ with each other in similar fight
styles, we get hooked, entangled and baited into a hassle.
We bait each other, we hook each other's needs, we dance
together. The similarities of our individual dance patterns
connect, coordinate and then collide. We get into symmetrical (similar) positions of blaming/feeling blamed then
defending/feeling accused followed by explaining/feeling
lectured or withdrawing/feeling distant. The paired combi-
nations are individually tailored by our inherited fight pat-

terns from the family of origin yet become remarkably similar after a few years together.

However, the first few years are most frequently characterized by a pattern of avoiding differences in order to establish and maintain the primary bond between the two. This denial frequently lasts for five to seven years before the real drive to eliminate the differences is expressed in the second marriage-within-a-marriage. This passage from the first marriage into the second is recognized in popular idiom. As Carl Whitaker, one of the most insightful family therapists notes:

"Nowadays, most marriages pass through serial impasses. The 10-year syndrome or the 7-year itch are both indications of our social concern with this kind of lock between two individuals and two states of being."[1]

"The 7-year itch" signals the rise in anxiety that ushers in "the 10-year syndrome" of reconsidering one's choice of partner, revising one's expectations and renegotiating the marital contract. If, that is, the relationship has sufficient durability and integrity to weather the storms that accompany the stormy passage between marriages. Seven years into marriage, most people are also dealing with leaving behind the youthful security of their 20s ("I'm still finding myself, my way; I'm free to experiment and explore") and entering their 30s ("I'm in the middle of my own life now; I'm the adult generation; I have to take final responsibility for my life and destiny.)

Authority is internalized as full responsibility and accepted in the 30s. Parents become peers, children reveal their inner natures so that a person discovers himself/herself through their eyes and actions. My new vision of the self initiates a different view of the marital partner. Life looks different, decade by decade, and each transition triggers either disruption of a marriage or new discovery of why we married and what we can become with and for each other.

"At 20, I thought we would accept each other freely, and obviously, totally. In the warmth of early love such unconditional appreciation of each other seemed so utterly inevitable and right. But by 30 I was at a very different place. I felt I had already adjusted to the limit of my flexibility, and I wanted some change from my spouse."

People change—if they are welcoming growth—and so the marriage must evolve as well. However, the need for security while making personal change may lead people to resist marital change. Inevitably, three different growth processes are simultaneously unfolding, interweaving and intermeshing—yours, mine and ours.

> Not only are each wife and each husband moving through an individual process of adult growth and change, connected to the passage of time and the successively shifting circumstances of adult life, but the marriage itself is undergoing similar periodic challenges and demands for adaptive change. A good way of conceptualizing this is to think in terms of *his* life cycle, *her* life cycle, and the marital cycle as a kind of supraentity—a whole which is more than and different from the sum of the two intimate partners involved in it. The *relationship itself* goes through a series of sequential phases, has its own set of internal dynamics and its own ongoing agenda.[2]

My personal struggle for identity, my discovery of central values and life commitments evolves decade by decade, as does yours. Each of us has a life to live, not as isolated individuals, but as centered responsible persons. And our marriage has a life of its own. It is composed not only of the contributions from our lives, but also from our families of origin, our sustaining community of co-travelers, our children and their respective worlds of individual development, and our connectedness to the Community of the Spirit (the Church) and the faith, hope and love that directs our pilgrimage together. The marriage is "bigger than both of us," "more than the sum of its parts," "a third presence when we are together," "a third body."

Poet Robert Bly speaks of this relationship as a "third body," which is prized by, precious to, separate from, yet continuous with each partner. Two become one without loss of their two-ness in the oneness that unites them. The marriage is not owned by either but shared by both; not dominated by one but expressive of each; not possessed by the couple but jointly owned by couple and community; not responsible only to each other but also with those who are connected to them historically, biologically, socially, legally, spiritually.

So he pursues his own developmental journey through the male life cycle. The stages of his life unfold from childhood, youth and young adulthood toward integrity as a man. He is becoming a human with maturity.

So she travels her unique developmental path through the life cycle as a woman. Her life unfolds period by period through character formation (childhood), personality formation (latency), identity formation (youth) into maturity as a woman. She is becoming a person of integrity.

Both continue to develop in the decades of growth—30s, 40s, 50s, 60s and 70s. This growth may be supported and stimulated by the marriage or may stunt and stifle their becoming their mature selves.

The marriage has a life cycle of its own. It must mature

from the naivete of early bonding through the storms or silence of early adjustment into middle marriage with its reconstruction and transformations until maturity in the relationship becomes possible.

The anxiety aroused by change in either the other or in the relationship may be paralyzing. There is no guarantee that the other will be there when needed or be what is needed. The risk of giving up what is known to venture into the unknown is a necessary condition for growth, but such giving up to move up, such dying to be reborn is never easy.

Accommodate

"If we don't talk about, don't even notice annoyances, they pass. And we get along. We adjust. We learn to overlook the differences. That's what love is about—accepting the other person no matter what."

If I grew up in a family where parents never fought, I will be very anxious when feelings erupt. *To love is to overlook.*

If I come from a home with chronic conflict, I may be conflict-shy. *To love is to absorb.*

If I am from a family where feelings, thoughts and actions were tightly controlled, I may inhibit my feelings totally. *To love is to inhibit.*

If I was raised in a family where agreement was demanded, then for me, to differ is to reject. *To love is to agree.*

If I grew up with people who felt obligated to read each other's minds and know each other's wants, then I will try to understand without communicating. *To love is to mind-read.*

THE HARMONIC THIRD

A third presence
    walks with us
    works with us
    talks with us.
    It is the we,
    The we we are becoming.

A third center
    connects us
    corrects us
    directs us.
    It is the we,
    The we we are discovering.

A third personhood
    unites us
    excites us
    lights us.
    It is the we,
    The we we are embracing.

In this third personhood
    of relationship
    we blend without fusing our selves
    we merge without losing our selves
    we become one by choosing each other.[3]

If I began life where conformity was necessary for people to accept and feel accepted, then I will try to fit perfectly with your wishes. *To love is to be pleasing.*

If I come from a home where loyalty demanded that we see no evil, say no evil, hear no evil about those we love, then I will deny all negative thoughts or feelings. *Love is denial.*

All these patterns of accommodation snooker persons into pretending to be in unison with each other when either dissonance or harmony would be much more appropriate. The ability to differ affectionately on trivial issues is learned by most persons early in life, but the capacity to tolerate deep differences, to live with ambiguity, to accept confusion is a sign of real maturity and emotional health. To appreciate such confusion in a marriage partner or in the marriage requires some years of growth. Early marriage, with the many impulses toward fulfilling the commands from the family of origin, tends to frighten us into accommodation. The accumulation of feelings that results from suppressing one's real emotions while "adjusting" to each other's preferences creates tensions that then break out in surprising and puzzling ways.

Accommodation, as the first stage of marriage, assists us in bonding with each other; it also insists on blinding us to each other's uniqueness and specialness.

1. *Bonding:* As the two persons begin to care for each other, attraction and affection and availability draw them together:

Attraction, the mysterious chemistry of history and biology, emotionality and rationality, need and novelty is as much an unconscious magnetism as it is conscious decision. We are drawn to the other by deep personality trends as well as the obvious similarities and differences that both reassure and excite us.

Forms Of "Love" That Call Us To Accommodate

Love is agreement.

If you love me,
do not differ.
To differ is to reject.

Love is conformity.

If you love me,
seek to please me.
Approval is everything.

Love is denial.

If you love me,
see, hear, say no evil.
Pretending is loyalty.

Love is control.

If you love me,
do what I want.
Act as I prescribe.

Love is obligation.

If you love me,
you owe me obedience.
Respect is your duty.

Love is rescuing.

If you love me,
let me rescue you.
I am your savior.

Love is togetherness.

If you love me,
you will always be
supportive
and never feel distant.

Love is anxiety.

If you love me,
you will fear what I fear.
Always feel what I feel.

Each of these forms of love is conditional. It is love given if one conforms, when one performs, because one lives by another's demands. Such love is unloving, because the heart-prizing, caring, valuing the other equally with the self is missing.

Affection, the warmth of feeling connected to another, turns the magnetism into attachment. The other person's wants and needs begin to compete with and complement our own.

Availability, the arranging of one's life, schedule, priorities to be there for the other and with the other gives the bond tangible, measurable, reliable connections. The bond of love is spelled T-I-M-E, and the availability of the other is the unmistable evidence of caring. All three of these elements of caring require creative accommodation.

In attraction, we are drawn to parts of the other that excite us while overshadowing those parts which will come into focus later. In affection, we gladly adjust to the other's wishes and wants in return for the rewards of warmth and acceptance. In the pledging of availability, we accommodate schedule, adjust life-style, align personal preferences, attune our priorities.

Later we may reconsider the accommodating choices, but in early bonding, the inflexible becomes flexible. The previously nonnegotiable is open to negotiation. We bond, all the way to our solid-self core. The pseudo-self, the negotiable second-hand part of the personality, interlocks with the other person's surface-self. Since the ratio of pseudo-self to solid self is very high, and the development of solid self progresses slowly, the bonding in the first stage allows for deep interpenetration of both personalities. Solid self is formed slowly from within; it is composed of deeply held, nonnegotiable values that lie at the core of the person. The more solid self, the more personhood; the more core solidity, the more integrity.

In the average person, the level of solid self is relatively low in comparison with the level of pseudo-self. A pseudo-self can function well in most relationships; but in an intense emotional relationship, such as marriage, the pseudo-self of one merges with the pseudo-self of the other. One becomes the functional self and the other a functional no-self.[4]

In early marriage, the two pseudo-selves do become one, temporarily. As the two become one it is only a matter of time until it becomes evident one may become dominant, the other eclipsed or both may struggle to reclaim the self-definition lost in the union.

2. *Blinding.* Accommodation inevitably blinds the person to much of the other because each of us is already oblivious to much of the self. Since I only come to know myself truly in relation to another, marriage is the natural cultural process for self-discovery, co-therapy, and mutual growth. As the unaware becomes aware, each has the privilege of discovery and the promise of depth in his or her own personal development.

The diagram of figure 1 offers a picture of this process. The two basic dimensions of understanding self and understanding the other are visualized as a window with four quadrants. The principles of change in marital discovery are as follows.

1. A change in any one quadrant will affect all the others. When one partner discloses something new about the self (reducing facade), all other quadrants change.
2. It takes energy to hide, deny or be blind to behavior, feelings, values or fears that are a part of your inner life, and, thus, also of the marriage.
3. Threat (anxiety) tends to decrease awareness, but mutual trust increases awareness. Any forced expo-

sure is usually ineffective. Gentle feedback and invitation to openness are most helpful.

4. The smaller the open arena, the less in common, the poorer the communication. Any experience of interpersonal learning increases the arena and decreases one or more of the other quadrants.

5. Being sensitive to one's partner means respecting what is hidden, blind or unknown and honoring the other's choice to keep it that way as long as is necessary.

6. The greater the area of open free activity, the more productive, creative, celebrative the marriage will be. Denial marriages have fixed quadrants; growing marriages have a continuing growth in the open arena.

7. The values of a marriage are seen in the way the two people handle the unknown areas of each other's lives. In early marriage, partners tend to accommodate to and protect the unknown. In middle marriage they may confront too harshly or expose themselves only under pressure. In later marriage they join in mutual self-discovery and fascinated exploration of the other. [5]

Emerging from the accommodation marriage, a couple finds they can no longer contain what they have concealed, and they cannot resist sharing what they know. Each couple finds its own way to explore the unknown or to flee it. Some retreat into a false togetherness of frozen accommodation—a pseudomutuality of niceness, tactfulness and protectiveness. Others flee into separation—a quiet, cold co-existence or distance and divorce. Both are exaggerated ways of totally eliminating the threat of the unknown in self and/or other. A divorce is invariably an attempt to escape oneself and to find oneself.

Shall we eliminate all stress by withdrawing into denial? Or into divorce? Or shall we eliminate the stres-

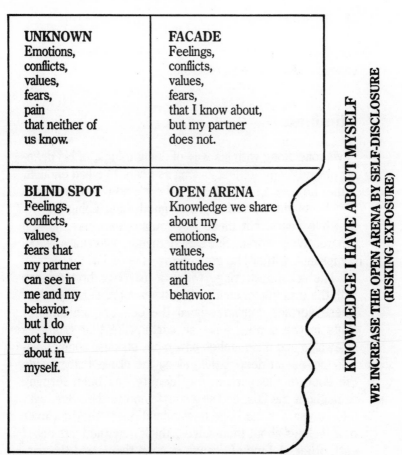

| UNKNOWN
Emotions,
conflicts,
values,
fears,
pain
that neither of
us know. | FACADE
Feelings,
conflicts,
values,
fears,
that I know about,
but my partner
does not. |
| BLIND SPOT
Feelings,
conflicts,
values,
fears that
my partner
can see in
me and my
behavior,
but I do
not know
about in
myself. | OPEN ARENA
Knowledge we share
about my
emotions,
values,
attitudes
and
behavior. |

KNOWLEDGE I HAVE ABOUT MYSELF

WE INCREASE THE OPEN ARENA BY SELF-DISCLOSURE
(RISKING EXPOSURE)

KNOWLEDGE MY PARTNER HAS ABOUT ME

WE INCREASE THE OPEN ARENA BY CONFRONTATION
(GIVING FEEDBACK)

Fig. 1. The Jo-hari Window and Marriage[6]

sors by confronting, demanding, pressuring the partner to change and live as we prescribe?

Eliminate

"I've gone along with his way of doing things, of his defining our relationship, just as long as I can. I've had enough. Either he meets me halfway or there's no way to go on."

"I thought we had a pretty good thing going for the first five years, but these last couple years have gotten progressively worse. She's all demands, all criticisms, all complaints. Either she gets off my case or I'm through."

The second marriage within a marriage breaks open with the eruption of conflict that has a more serious edge: These surface conflicts signal the deeper rumblings of shifts in the depths. Like an earthquake that crumples sidewalks and mismatches pavement stripes, conflict signals movement deep within, along the plates that provide the floor of the personality. Identity has been forming throughout the 20s, and as a couple enters their 30s, with 5 to 10 years of marriage now behind them, they discover new feelings about themselves, think new thoughts about each other. A time of change is upon them, and the passage from the first marriage to the second is marked by storms in some couples, by a cold winter for others, by significant change in all.

The differences that frustrate or confuse look like irritants that must be eliminated. Demands for changes in the other person rise from surprisingly deep feeling levels. Expectations of what a marriage partner should offer have been disappointed; fears of what a partner might become have been fulfilled. Change seems to be not only in order, but absolutely necessary if the relationship is to continue.

Family therapist, James Framo writes of this time of desperation:

"The secret agendas of marriage partners defy reality. People make impossible demands on marriage, based on the idea that one's spouse should make one happy. No one can make this work. It is not possible to go through life, with or without a partner, without experiencing some pain and loneliness. Yet people act as if their spouses *owe* them happiness as an inalienable right. You can't make anyone love you, and no one can make you happy."[7]

Conflict and change bring about a time of high anxiety. The security of our love is breaking up. The possibility of separation or, even worse, of lifeless co-existence is deeply troubling.

"I married the wrong person," one begins to fear. The misfit in the marriage and the contrast in personal needs all become foreground. The burnout of the old commitment to accommodate leaves a fatigue with repeating old cycles, an exasperation and impatience with familiar irritants, an edginess on failed expectations and an elemental sense of disappointment.

Disappointment with the other person springs up first. He is too wrapped up in his work. She is too invested in her career. He expects the family to adjust to his needs but he is inflexible when others need him. She is much more excited by work relationships and friendships than by the failing marriage.

"I've chosen the wrong person, with the wrong ideas about love and relationship," one begins to conclude. The idea forms that some people are incompatible for reasons that are unchangeable and indisputable. Incompatibility is more an attitude than a condition; it is a state that people create, not a trait that is beyond change. It is a sign of deep disappointment with another person that has turned toward despair.

Disappointment with oneself emerges later. "How have I failed the marriage? How have I been the wrong person in this relationship? How have I failed to be the partner I might have been? Questions such as these lurk in the back of the mind, haunting each person with the sense of failure.

The constant temptation is to focus the anger on the other person's failure, but the constant irritation is the recognition that every criticism of the other is a confession about the self. Every fault one sees in the partner is a fault in the viewer as well as the one viewed. When one observes a fault in the other that rankles and irritates, that is an undeniable sign that the other's fault is one's own, too.

In reality, we marry the right person—far more right than we can know. In a mysterious, intuitive, perhaps instinctive fashion we are drawn by both similarities and differences, by needs and anxieties, by dreams and fears to choose our complement, our reflection in another.

We always marry the right person, and the discovery of that rightness moves us into the third marriage within a marriage. We at last begin to appreciate what we had sought to eliminate.

Appreciate

"It was, in some unexplainable way, like falling in love again. The very things I had come to resent in her, I realized I needed. In fact, I no longer resented them, I was fulfilled by them."

These words are very personal. I have spoken them

You Always Marry
The Wrong Person

You didn't really know
what you thought you knew
when you did what you did
and said what you said.
You didn't know what you needed
or what you needed to know
to choose who you chose
so you can't see what you saw.

You Always Marry
The Right Person

Although you didn't really know
what you thought you knew,
you really did know
what you needed to know
when you did what you did.
You knew more than you knew,
you did better than you would
had you known what you didn't.

myself, I have heard them from wives and husbands rediscovering each other at mid-life. I have seen the returning
sparkle of affection, felt the renewed warmth in relationship as appreciation welcomes what frustration had been
seeking to eliminate.

What we appreciate in another we invariably resent as
well, and what we resent reveals the hidden appreciation.
But often the two feelings struggle to eclipse or eliminate
each other—resentment overwhelms the appreciation,
frustration obliterates the admiration. A man marries a
woman with a capacity to listen and give faithful attention,
yet he soon discovers resentment of her silence. She
chooses a man with warm articulate expressiveness yet
quickly becomes exhausted with his flood of words. He
loved and then hated her ears; she was attracted to and
then repulsed by his mouth.

One loves the outer world of experience and draws
energy from its excitement and stimulation; the other is
energized by the inner world of ideas and reflection. The
extrovert then comes to resent the introvert's hidden-
ness; the introvert is repulsed by the extrovert's superfi-
ciality.

As we each discover that we knew more than we knew
when we chose whom we chose, appreciation begins to
break into a gentle flame. In appreciation, we discover that
people who marry each other *reflect* each other. There is a
similar level of maturity, a parallel set of self-
understandings and self-acceptance in most couples
choosing each other. The two express their self-image and
self-valuation in the person selected.

People who marry each other *complete* each other in a
puzzling yet pronounced way. The missing is supplied, the
imbalanced is brought into equilibrium, the dormant is
enriched by what is dominant in the other.

People who marry each other *deserve* each other. If the interlocking traits had not existed, there would not have been that unique fit that is felt as love. He was what she was missing, she had him coming; he lacked what she boasted; he got what he deserved.

Although done in humor, these words reveal a truth about marriage which can only be said tongue in cheek. In the appreciation stage of marriage we recover a sense of humor that got eliminated during the previous period.

PEOPLE WHO MARRY EACH OTHER *REFLECT* EACH OTHER:

I see myself
as loved and lovable
in the other's eyes.
My self-esteem,
my ability to love
are expressed in my choice
and in my being chosen.

PEOPLE WHO MARRY EACH OTHER *COMPLETE* EACH OTHER:

What is missing in one
is supplied in the other,
what is immature in one
is balanced by the other,
what is dominant in one
lies dormant in the other.

PEOPLE WHO MARRY EACH OTHER
DESERVE EACH OTHER:

We were that way
to begin with
or we would not have fit.
We became that way
from living with each other
or we would not have
survived.

SO BLAME IS POINTLESS:
IT ALL COMES OUT EVEN.

Now we can chuckle at what previously seemed so
serious. The line between tragedy and comedy is incredi-
bly thin. The same data, earlier seen through angry eyes
as tragic, now appears as comedic. With the return of a
true sense of humor, appreciation of the other person—
warts and all—is celebrated.

"I look back at things we used to hassle, I remember
what they were, but I forget why. If I had eliminated the
differences in my mate or given up my own, it would have
been a real loss."

Celebrate

The fourth marriage within a marriage breaks as a couple
begins to celebrate the differences which once antago-
nized them. What they originally tolerated in an attempt to

accommodate and later sought to eliminate, they both appreciate and celebrate now because their uniqueness has become essential to each.

This period of depth-relationship opens as the partners find that the quirks and foibles, the preferences and the pet peeves of the other are not only understandable, they add to the other's specialness and preciousness.

In a less mature period, a husband may struggle to remake his wife, as a wife may wish for a husband who will seek to live as she would prescribe; now all that is utterly undesirable. The mature capacity to prize the differences that attract and complete the relationship brings a halt to the old strategies of playing therapist or teacher or coach.

Humor takes different forms and serves a different function in this marriage. Now it is a celebrative humor of acceptance rather than a prickly humor which serves as a nudge as much as a chuckle. Now jousting turns to jesting, prodding to playing.

The two welcome conflict as an occasion for growth. Where their hope once was to manage the conflict, they now seek to utilize it to hear each other more clearly, understand each other more fully, know each other more intimately.

Embracing conflict as a positive part of loving and growing takes away the sting which once went with the clash of wills. During this later period, women tend to become more assertive, men more affiliative. The tendency to accept the limitations imposed on women by oppressive cultural norms is wearing out, and the 40s and 50s become a time for claiming one's power to ask for what one needs, stand for what one believes and press for what one wants. Males who suppressed their tender feelings, denied their dependencies and kept their weaknesses hidden behind a show of strength, now begin to recognize their needs for more acceptant, affirming and nurturant relationships.

When a couple has matured into their fourth marriage by this age, these movements in opposite directions do not pass each other by, but bring them together. Seeing the opposite sides of the other person, experiencing the newness of reversal in relationships as personalities are inverted is a cause for playful, often joyful, celebration. The two enjoy each other and enjoy each other's enjoyment of their new ways of responding.

This enjoyment of being enjoyed is what celebration is about. I delight in your differences; you delight in mine; I find your delight delightful as you do mine. Joy requires a complete circuit. One may experience pleasure alone, but joy is relational, cyclical, reciprocal, a mutually rewarding interaction, intercourse and intertwining of spirit and body, of thought and feeling. In every stage of marriage are moments of celebration, but the depth of delight in our differentness and our similarity, our contrast and our commonality comes with the maturity of the persons and the maturing of the relationship.

EXERCISE 2: THE MANAGEMENT OF DIFFERENCES _____

Instructions. To get a clearer picture of your most frequent way of handling differences, complete the following inventory. Although none of the options will match your own response accurately, try to choose the one which is most typical of your responses and give it a score of 5. The other responses should be scored in order of preference from the most likely (5) to least likely (1). You will assign a sequential number to each although there may be wider differences in your preference for or rejection of a particular response.

Instructions: rank the following responses from 1 to 5, with *one* given to the least acceptable option and *five* to the most preferred response.

1. There are times when you would really like for your partner to do something for you or plan something with you.

   _____ a. You say what you want clearly and ask if the other is open to doing it or would rather not participate.

   _____ b. You know in advance which way he or she is most likely to lean, so you try to expect what is in line with your past experiences.

   _____ c. You tell the other person to do it in an open demand with a tone that warns of a coming hassle if the other refuses or postpones.

   _____ d. You hint around and hope he or she will sense what you want, if he loves you, or she cares about your wishes.

   _____ e. You bring up the subject casually to test the waters and get an idea of how the other will react.

2. Sometimes you disagree over what to do on an evening out, on which restaurant to choose or on who you want to invite to join you.

   _____ a. You don't make a fuss; you go along with your partner's plans to keep peace.

   _____ b. You suggest that you both figure out something you would equally enjoy together.

   _____ c. You decide that, if there is any disagreement, you would rather not do anything tonight.

_____d. You report how strongly you feel about your preference, check out how strongly your partner is committed and seek a compromise by coming partway.

_____e. You point out what is wrong with your partner's suggestion and defend your own strongly as the much better option.

3. You feel very angry about something your partner said or did that feels like a blunder, an attack or a slight.

_____ a. You try to get your mind off of it and busy yourself in other things without mentioning how you feel.

_____ b. You find a mutually acceptable time to go for a walk together, where you can report your anger feelings and explain why you feel as you do and what you want.

_____ c. Without letting on that you are at all angry, you ask indirect questions about the other's actions and motives.

_____ d. You blow up at the next thing he or she says and tell what an insensitive action this was and then unload.

_____ e. You comment that there may have been feelings building up between you and suggest that you set aside time to each clear the air if there are any problems and then, if the other shares, you share yours.

4. Sometimes the other person seems moody or down in

the dumps about something that is frustrating or depressing.

_____ a. You tell him or her it's time to stop moping and get a more positive outlook.
_____ b. You try to distract your mate and see if you can't cheer the other up.
_____ c. You say you are concerned and ask what is wrong and where your mate is hurting.
_____ d. You say you are open to talk about it, if the other wants to discuss what's happening.
_____ e. You respect the other's feelings and go on about your own work and life until he or she comes around.

5. Sometimes you have strong feelings about a decision, and feel that the other person's point of view is wrong.

_____ a. You decide that nothing is worth a major confrontation, you'll go along this time to keep the relationship more smooth.
_____ b. You tell your partner what you believe in no uncertain terms and demand cooperation this time.
_____ c. You suggest that the two of you spend time exploring other options, so that no one wins or loses and a mutually satisfactory solution emerges, if possible.
_____ d. You offer a solution that comes halfway to meet the other and invite him or her to do the same.
_____ e. You postpone a decision in the hope that time will help the other person to come to see it your way.

6. You are worried about something to the point that it is affecting your feelings toward your mate.

    _____ a. You go on acting as if nothing is bothering you, so it won't cause even more stress.

    _____ b. You don't let on that you are worried, but you bring up the subject to see if the other shares any of your feelings.

    _____ c. You become edgy and uptight and see if you can bring out similar feelings in the other, so you can share the problem together.

    _____ d. You tell the partner that you are worried, share your concerns and ask for the support you need.

    _____ e. You point out that the other isn't concerned at all about how you feel and has been ignoring your feelings.

7. Your partner does something that pleases you very much; you are delighted with his or her actions.

    _____ a. You say how pleased you are and thank the other for what your mate did and for who that person is.

    _____ b. You feel, "I better enjoy this while I can; he or she will probably never do it again; besides it's more than I deserve."

    _____ c. You keep your feelings to yourself and don't mention it.

    _____ d. You thank the other for doing what he/she did and look for a way to even the score by doing something nice for him/her.

    _____ e. You report how good it was he or she did

this, point out it could have been done before and should be from now on.

8. You are impatient with your partner's slowness in fulfilling an agreed upon promise or task.

_____ a. You get it off your chest and tell him or her how the postponing makes you angry.

_____ b. You decide it's not your problem, if the other can live with it, so can you.

_____ c. You try to be extra nice to the other and help your partner with his/her overload, hoping this will hurry the person along.

_____ d. You offer to do something for your partner if he/she in turn will carry out the previous agreement.

_____ e. You discuss the problem, the schedule and your feelings openly and ask how you can support a better resolution than just letting it ride.

To score your responses, enter your selection by letter in the appropriate column.

1.	a___	e___	d___	c___	b___
2.	b___	d___	a___	e___	c___
3.	b___	e___	c___	d___	a___
4.	c___	d___	b___	a___	e___
5.	c___	d___	a___	b___	e___
6.	d___	c___	b___	e___	a___
7.	a___	d___	b___	e___	c___
8.	e___	d___	c___	a___	b___
TOTAL	___	___	___	___	___
	Collaboration	Compromise	Accommodation	Compelling	Avoidance

Collaboration: A high score on collaboration indicates a strong preference for seeking mutually satisfactory solutions. It values openness, honesty and direct conversation to work through differences in goal without sacrificing differences in personality and perspective.

Compromise: A high score in compromise shows a willingness to meet the other halfway and work out a joint solution which combines a part of each person's desires. It values both persons' needs, but is willing to yield something to gain something.

Accommodation: A high score suggests a tendency to yield one's goals in order to maintain relationship. It places high emphasis on supportive relationship sustained even through sacrifice and peace at any price.

Compelling: A high score shows a tendency to use force to compel cooperation. It reveals a preference for being in control, for win-lose behavior. The compeller insists on being right, and identifying the other as wrong.

Avoidance: A high score indicates a tendency to avoid conflict, withdraw from confrontation and let time and circumstance resolve or dissolve differences.

The five responses can be viewed as ways of combining the two basic needs in all marriages—the need for connectedness and relationship, and the need for achieving one's goals and fulfilling values. This provides the five options and shows their different ratios of commitment to either caring or confronting, or the combination of both in collaboration.

The preferred scores are, in order: to work toward collaboration if possible; to move back to compromise for a while, if necessary; to accept accommodation as third choice and use compelling as fourth and last; avoidance should be used rarely, if at all.

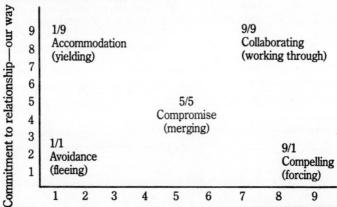

Compare your scores, and talk about how you are working to improve joint collaboration and effective compromise. All other solutions should be temporary until the couple can move back to seek mutually satisfactory solutions.

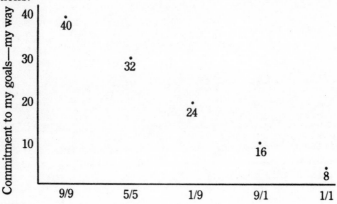

3

GOALS

DREAM—DISILLUSIONMENT—
DISCOVERY—DEPTH

We marry to fulfill the Dream—personal, marital, vocational and communal dreams.

The Dream fails us—or we sacrifice the marital dream to gain the career dream or some other dream.

We discover reality beyond the Dream; we discover each other.

We develop depth in ourselves, our marriage, our life together.

Jill

"I want excitement. John is totally predictable. I think it was boredom that drove me to the affair. The dream that we used to share had disappeared.

"I never intended to hurt my husband. But I did want some response, some sign of life from him. His silence felt like abandonment, his patience was like passivity to me. I wanted to feel something, to be alive again.

"When I began going to lunch with another man, he didn't seem to notice. Soon we were skipping lunch and going to his apartment, but John asked no questions. Even when he found a love letter, he didn't get emotional. He just said no one would ever care for me as much as he did.

"When we married seven years ago, we had everything I'd dreamed about. Affection, excitement, passion. He made me feel so special, so loved. He'd come home at lunch to seduce me. We were always together; we resented the time we had to be apart.

"Now he has only energy enough for the practice of dentistry, and lots of time for our daughter, but we've grown apart. When I think about his distant silence, I feel anger flaming all through me."

John

"I love Jill's energy and excitement. She is the color in my black-and-white world. I try to keep up with her changes, but this is too much. I've gone on quietly even when she became attracted to another man, but I've had all I can take.

"I've no idea why Jill is unhappy with our marriage or why she is involved with someone else. I've given her the constant love and faithfulness I think she deserves. What more can I give?

"We were close our first three years. I was in dental school, she was finishing art school. We had lots of time to play. But then I began my practice and she became pregnant. We had to work to reach our dream. Just when everything was beginning to fit together she pulled it all apart. I've tried to go on being loving and understanding, but there's a limit to anything. When I think of her in bed with this Jim, I go crazy. I've not said anything to push her away, but I've had it."

Seven years into the marriage, the Dream is fading, the marriage is dying. Perhaps being reborn. One marriage ends, will another begin?

> Marriage is the pursuit of a dream.
> A dream of loving and being loved;
> of wanting another and being wanted in return,
> of melting into another and being eagerly embraced,
> of understanding another and being understood,
> of feeling secure and guaranteeing another's security,
> of being fulfilled in fulfilling another's needs.

But the Dream, like all dreams, is shaped by the minor themes that may enrich or impoverish the central melody of love. These themes, subtle or blatant, may contain strands

> of dominating or being dominated,
> of rescuing or being rescued,
> of being parent or being parented,
> of seeking justice for past injustices,

of atoning for past tragedies or mistakes,
of being able to express uncensored feelings,
of feeling free to be what was forbidden by others.

The themes of our dreams are as varied as our individuality, as tangled as our families of origin, as complex as
the needs we bring—aware and unaware—to the altar
and the marriage bed.

Marriage is born even before the fantasies and dreams
that begin in our childhood relationships with those who
first teach us to give love and to receive it; actually, one's
marriage is rooted in the marriages of parents and grandparents. The Dream is caught early, it is taught uncon-
sciously in the context of the family of origin.

The Dream of a special, a unique, a one-of-a-kind-
in-the-whole-world man is forming in the girl and emerges
in the woman. The Dream of the perfect woman who will
embody, excite, fulfill, express all that is feminine is
already forming in the infant boy's first moment of being
pressed to the mother's breast.

In reality, the Dream never begins, it continues from
the family of origin, extending the individual dreams of
family members and the collective dream of the family
mythology. I express my family's hopes, values, fears,
expectations. As I have become a person of responsible
choice, I have altered, reshaped, resisted and recreated
parts of that dream.

Yet, I discover on closer examination, much more continues than I see in casual survey of present behavior or
future plans. In more careful review of the past, the family
dreams appear, the similarities across generations snap
into focus, the continuities emerge, either in the ways I
have repeated old expectations or have reacted in reverse
directions. My parents' marriage, as well as the marriages

of grandparents I never knew, are affecting my own. I am enriched by and constricted by ways of behaving that are complex patterns assembled from a variety of marriages before me and learned by admiration and imitation as well as by resistant reaction and resentful repetition.

What we resist persists. What we resent we often repeat. What we react against we tend to reproduce. What we fear we may actually help create out of our overreaction, our rigidity, our inability to choose freely. So the romantic dream of marriage that draws us into intimacy and loving relationship is shadowed by darker dreams that are fearful, resentful and undeniably powerful.

The dream of marriage each of us projects on the screen of the one we love is actually a cluster of dreams, positive *and* negative, chosen *and* caught, joyfully fantasized *and* cautiously feared. This richly varied dream world arises from both the near and distant past to compose the tapestry of emotions, perceptions and actions of the new marriage.

As two join in life together, it's dreamtime.

Marriage is not the only dream, it flows along with the other central dreams—of career and life work, of success and communal esteem, of happiness in meaningful celebration of loving, working and living with others. Our family and culture suggest which dream will predominate—marriage, parenthood, profession, personhood—and which dreams will be subordinated, sacrificed or ignored. Often the *Dream* emerges as a blend of "all of the above" without consciously chosen priorities.

The Dream

The first hints of the Dream appear in the fantasies, games

and play of childhood. The dreams of our parents and siblings are visible all around us, offering pathways for our
own dreams. The family's work, play, possessions and
passion for life express the family dream that we inherit.
Out of the richness or the poverty of the family dream we
begin to image our own future.

THE DREAMERS

A man and a woman,
young and beautiful,
drawn by passion
and physical attraction,
are overwhelmed by
tender thoughts,
constant longing,
erotic feelings,
a need to be
with the other at all
times.
Captivated by a dream
obsessed to addiction,
willing to risk all
to fulfill their love,
they scorn reason,
laugh at harsh realities,
stand alone against the
world,
ignoring others'
objections,
believing in their destiny
to be loving forever.

> In love with each other,
> in love with being loved,
> in love with love,
> each believes the other
> can fulfill the Dream:
> she will be his dream,
> he will become hers.

Adolescent ambitions and youthful fantasies excite us with the possibilities of life beyond the family's horizons. The Dream, as it emerges, is necessarily idealistic, it is larger than life, beyond one's talents. All is possible, all will work out, the unexpected will happen, the big break will come.

As the Dream develops, it narrows. Each choice eliminates options. Each step limits the directions open and the Dream is reshaped into a personal identity with choices of career, education, place of living, relationships, success, marriage, family, home, play and avocations.

The Dream always represents *one part* of oneself. The pursuit of the Dream demands the loss or sacrifice of the parts of the self that cannot be realized or included in the pursuit of the goal. The Dream not only has external costs of time, effort, risk, it also has internal costs of undeveloped options, talents, preferences and values. "The road not taken" will continue to echo down the road one takes.

Originally, the Dream is a vague sense of what is possible, a poorly articulated vision of what can be which is only tenuously connected to reality. Gradually the Dream becomes clearly visualized and sharply articulated in the person's thoughts. Throughout the educational journey the Dream serves as the lure. For some it is explicitly stated as a life goal. For others it is implicit, a gentle nudge from within that is not allowed to surface fully or be stated frankly.

If one becomes a physicist or biologist, the Dream may point to the Nobel prize. For a journalist or writer, the Dream may focus on the Pulitzer. For the athlete, the artist, the attorney, the business executive, the Dream has its own shape, style and rewards.

THE DREAM

may be modest
or heroic,
vaguely defined
or crystal clear,
a burning passion
or a quiet guiding force,
a source of inspiration and
strength
or of corrosive conflict.
My life is enriched
to the extent that
I have a Dream
and give it
appropriate place
in my life
—a place
that is legitimate
and viable
for both myself
and my world.
If I have no Dream
or can find no way

to live it out
my life lacks
genuine purpose
or meaning.[1]

Marriage and the Dream

The pursuit of the Dream is not a male or female preroga-
tive, but it has been exaggerated in male life-styles. Daniel
Levinson and associates described the functions of the
Dream in the life patterns of the 40 men they studied in
The Seasons of a Man's Life. What emerges is an unfortu-
nate pattern of workaholic husbands pursuing "the Great
American Dream," while their wives are left to cope with
the "petty realities of life."

This polarization creates a skewed marital contract
since a central assumption for such a man is that the wife
will help him achieve his Dream. This nurse-doctor marriage has no clear agreement on reciprocity. She may initially agree to help in exchange for security, status or
material goods, but later she discovers that the cost has
been greater than anticipated.

> If in supporting his dream she loses her own,
> then her development will suffer and both will
> later pay the price. Dynamics of this kind often
> surface in transitional periods such as the Age
> Thirty Transition or the Mid-life Transition.[2]

As the polarization of the marriage contract matures,
the workaholic husbands tend to present nice, reasonable,
pleasant facades, while the wives appear as bitchy, angry
or depressed.

For the husband, the Dream demands that he be

success-oriented, hard-driving, competitive and ambitious. Once the whole personality has been invested in the Dream, any failure to actualize it may lead to feelings of inadequacy and worthlessness, so he demands support, care and nurturance from his wife, and acceptance of his absence and preoccupation by the children.

> Components of this dream are enacted by the decision that to achieve this goal he will need courage, strength, and determination, as shown through the following characteristics: (a) reason and logic as the means through which the dream is achieved; (b) strength, courage, determination are demonstrated by keeping feelings to himself and repressing, denying and avoiding any expression of feelings that may possibly suggest vulnerability, weakness, or even worse inadequacy.[3]

The success-orientation demands that he put a great deal of effort in proper appearances and good first impressions. Clothing, car, house, spouse, children are exhibits one to five. The family's values are shaped by his need to present himself to his public in the best light possible.

For the wife, the Dream requires that she do all the work which family life requires and he neglects. Unaware of the trivia of day-to-day realities, he depends on her to carry out the entire nurturant task which belongs to both. Seemingly unaware of "mundane chores and trivial tasks," he pours all his efforts into the "important work" of success and facade. As she confronts him with these daily realities, his denial and avoidance provoke increased irritability and anger in her.

As the marriage polarizes in roles, the elusive Dream

becomes his life project, the hard reality of routine work falls to her. The more "nice" he becomes to his public, the more nasty she appears when she confronts him about neglecting family life. The more expressive she becomes about her feelings of isolation and alienation, the more inexpressive he appears in his denial of any problems at home.

If the Dream is within reach and success is rewarding his workaholism, then the gulf between his self-image and her view of him becomes greater. When he can no longer reconcile the discrepancy, he will frequently act out his frustration by becoming even more obsessed with work and success or he may broaden the work-affair to include a mistress, an addiction to the preferred substance or an obsession with golf, flying or spectator sports.

This traditional complementary pattern of Mr. Dream/ Mrs. Dreamer was restrictive to each and destructive of both. The executive dreamer who absorbs the assistant dreamer loses respect for self when exploiting as well as for the one who is exploited. The person who permits such absorption loses self-esteem and cannot esteem the other. Yet this pattern is the most common resolution to the role and relational conflicts of early marriage. It is shaped by the dream of making it socially, economically, vocationally in a success-oriented culture. And it is fired by romance—the mystical trust in emotional attraction and attachment to the "special other."

In a growing relationship, each partner becomes a "special" person i the drama of the Dream. The partner becomes a mentor of the Dream, seeking to animate, liberate, facilitate the part of the self that is nourished by the Dream. He welcomes her fulfilling of her dream; she invites him to pursue his vision. Both serve, at different times, as encourager, sponsor, critic, guide, motivater, listener. Each invites the other to discover both sides of the inner self—the masculine and the feminine poles of creativity. Each helps the other shape and live out the individual and the joint aspects of the Dream. Each shares in the vision, believes in the other as its hero, blesses the journey and welcomes the other back for nourishment and encouragement.

In past centuries, the Dream was the male prerogative, the "special woman" served as the anima, the supportive special person. Today each has an equal right to dream, each deserves and requires the support of the other. Neither identity dare be swallowed up in his or her own dream, and neither has the right to co-opt the other's identity to fulfill the dream.

Yet both of these mistakes—the total investing of one's own identity in the Dream, the usurping of the other's identity are extremely common. To live only for the Dream, to make it one's total life project is squandering the privilege of being fully alive with each other. To eclipse the partner in service of one's personal goals hampers the growth of both.

Romance and the Dream

> When we married seven years ago, we had everything I'd dreamed about. Affection, excitement, passion. He made me feel so special, so loved. He'd come home at lunch to seduce me. We were always together; we resented the time we had to be apart.

The dream of marriage is woven of the songs we learn to sing, the movies that excite us, the novels that captivate our imaginations, the life-styles of our star personalities, the values of our faith community and the character of our family life. In the Western family, the dominant theme throughout all of these is romance.

Romantic love is an intense over-estimation, an unconscious infatuation, a projective idealization that elevates another to an idolized place, in effect, by shielding the lover from the other's real face.

Romantic love was first sung by the twelfth-century troubadors in western Europe, practiced by courtiers who worshiped high-born ladies from afar, idealized in literature and drama and adopted as a cultural value in increasing circles of Western society.

Romantic love can be sustained by a knight who worships an inaccessible lady-love with continuous yearning but no hope of fulfillment. This unrequited love was prompted by fate, predestined by the power of "love" and considered beyond the control of rational thought. The knight—married to a wife of his social class—was capable of only extramarital love for this serendipitous lady—who was married in a traditional familial and political alliance.

This romantic ideal of love is an impossible foundation for a lifelong relationship. Denis de Rougemont, a historian of love, believes that romance offers no support at all. "We are in the act of trying out—and failing miserably at it, one of the most pathological experiments that a civilized society has ever imagined, namely, the basing of marriage, which is lasting, upon romance which is a passing fancy."[4]

Romantic love is for people who dream of one another from a distance, not for those who live together day after day. It is for those who long for union but can only bridge the separation through fantasy, whose fires of passion are excited by imagination but never cooled by consumation. The romantic ideal is easily fractured by reality, its mystic perfection cannot be matched by fallible human relationships.

Romantic love, rising as it does from earlier levels of the personality, places great faith in the unconscious. When love is "true love," I am supposed to feel *it* and know *it* when *it* hits like a lightning bolt. *It* overwhelms rational sense, overpowers objections, overcomes all obstacles. *It*—in Latin the word is *id*—is a deep and powerful impulse from within, an intuitive eruption from unconscious processes that flood the soul with a romantic vision of another.

In classic romanticism, from the Middle Ages on, the supreme passion which drives the person to yearn for the beloved contained an essential ingredient of search for an ultimate and tragic union which is possible only in death. Passion is suffering. Its fires are fed by the insurmountable obstacles which separate the lovers. It is the *search* that feeds the intense feelings, not the *finding;* it is the barriers that fire the obsession, not the attaining of infinite ecstatic bliss in togetherness. Such lovers were not in love with each other, but each was in love with love and in love with the passionate self with its urging blinding all-absorbing erotic passions.

The logical
and normal
outcome
of marriage
founded only
on romance,
   is divorce,
   for marriage
      kills
      romance;

If romance
reappears,
    it
    will
    kill
the marriage
by its incompatibility
with the very reasons
for which the marriage
was contracted.[5]

The myth of romantic love offers an unconscious chan-
nel for vicarious relief of those mysterious impulses
toward savage, passionate love which are feared because
one instinctively knows that such uncontrolled passion
would be destructive if it were lived out without restraint.
Romantic passion feeds on obstacles and difficulties that
lead inevitably toward pain, suffering and possible death if
pursued with unchecked intensity; it fires vicious cycles of
passionate pursuit, capture, disillusionment, divorce,
renewed pursuit and the like.[6]

The ideal of romantic love—the Dream—may draw us
toward marriage, but the real—the daily reality—
characterizes most of life together. Living with the discrepancy between the two often requires that dream and
reality be kept separate and distinct. The excitement of
the Dream, the exhaustion of the daily routine require one
to be both idealistic and practical, sensual and stoic, imagi-
native and mundane. Western culture teaches us to
believe in romantic love even while recognizing that relationships rarely work out that way. The picture we create
and the reality we discover match in moments of peak
experience but not in day-to-day encounter.

ROMANTIC LOVE

Romantic love is a fabric of interwoven, enmeshed expectations:

Admiration
Jill is in awe of everything Jack does. She is impressed by his appearance, intelligence, wit and wisdom.

Indulgence
Jack gives Jill everything a woman wants—diamonds and furs, a house and car, every wish or whim.

Control
Jill must know and approve of all Jack does. When he refuses to comply she cries that he doesn't love her. Jack can't stand to see her sad, so he yields to her control.

Exploitation
Jack takes advantage of Jill by assuming she will provide company, service, sex as it suits him. If something else comes up, he stands her up, but when it suits him he really loves her.

Obedience
Jill serves Jack's needs in every way possible. She adjusts to his emotional changes, provides for his physical needs, is more concerned for his sexual desires than her own.

Loyalty
Jack, in undying devotion to Jill, ignores any bad habits, overlooks any weaknesses and rises to her defense if anyone criticizes her in any way.

Consideration
Jill tries hard to never say an unkind word to Jack to protect his "fragile male ego." No matter how tired or taxed she is, his needs are always first.

Possessiveness
Jack demonstrates his love for Jill by jealousy. He loves her so much he can't bear the thought of her enjoying friendship or conversation with any other man.

Fidelity

Jack is Jill's one and only, sexually faithful since they fell in love.
As long as he is true to her bodily, that is all that matters.

Sexuality

Jack and Jill share sexual contact and release—at least for him.
They do not threaten this intimacy level by talking about feelings
or hopes, or pain and disappointment.

Romance

Jack and Jill are never so much in love as when alone with soft
music and candles and fond memories of the past—the day they
saw love reflected in each other's eyes.

Destiny

Jack and Jill will live happily ever after. Their love will conquer all
obstacles. They will never have to say, "I'm sorry." They were
made for each other.[7]

Romantic love is a fabric of interwoven, interlocking, enmeshed expectations. One admires the other,
and the other indulges in return. One lovingly con-
trols, the other lovingly exploits. One obeys to earn
love, the other protects and rewards. One is highly
possessive, the other loyal and faithful. Yet both place
such expectations on the other that all the above may
be reversed or exchanged in an intricate dance.
Because I admire my partner, I indulge her. She
returns the same consideration in a warm possessiveness. And all is understood as the expression of the
romantic love which is their destiny.

This fascinatingly intricate network of reciprocal
expectations thrives on the feelings of affection and
infatuation, on dependency and delight, on attachment
and fusion, on romance and a sense of destiny.

In the first marriage within a marriage, the Dream
of romance dominates the love given and received, but
by middle marriage the Dream has faltered. If it

remains, it is as servant to a more tough and resilient
love rather than as disillusioning tyrant. Most often as
the Dream breaks up, anxiety rises when both fear the
relationship is dying. Instead, the marriage may be
reborn in the passage from the first stage to the second.

Disillusionment

I've no idea why she is unhappy with our marriage. But I feel like the bottom has dropped out
of my world. I've worked hard to make our
dream come true, but now she's involved with
someone else. I don't want our marriage to fold,
but I've had it.

The Dream ends. Disillusionment takes its place. The
first marriage within a marriage is over. The second is
thrust upon the struggling pair.

Disillusioned with their dreams, the couple is also
struggling with the loss of illusions about their marriage
and about each other. Painful as it is to see dreams die,
even more difficult is to lose the loved image of the partner. The picture of the other which was tinted by
romance, retouched by loving loyalty and carefully illumi-
nated by fond memories now begins to fade, distort, dis-
appear. The real face appears, the authentic feelings are
expressed, the true self is seen. The beloved illusion is
being stripped away. Each must discover whether there is
a continuing love for the person when the old persona is
becoming transparent.

Couples who place a high value on appearance, performance or achievement may prefer the old persona to

the person that is emerging in middle marriage. The image is preferred to the reality. To have the image destroyed is to fall out of love, they believe. But the reverse is true. To discard the image and encounter the person is to discover love. Love is a discovery, rather than an achievement, action or feeling. When one discovers the other person's preciousness beyond their attractive self-presentation, their worth beneath their appearance, then authentic love emerges. But before the third stage of *discovery* can occur, one needs to bottom out in a time of *disillusionment*.

Disillusionment as Disappointment

In disillusionment, one becomes disappointed with the partner, with the marriage and with the self:

1. In disappointment with the partner is a deep sense of despair, a profound feeling of having been mistaken in one's choice of a mate. "I made the wrong choice, picked the wrong person for me. You do not fit my needs, dreams, personality.

2. In disappointment with the marriage is a generalized anger at the obligatory nature of the public covenant that holds us together and at our interpersonal covenant that has become so binding to us both. "I've expected more out of marriage than the other person is prepared to give. Either there's something wrong with marriage in general or with this one we've created in particular."

3. In disappointment with the self is anger that one has not been able to be the kind of partner that builds a successful relationship. "I should have been so effective as a wife/husband that this would not have happened. I wish I had been more clear, less ambiguous in my expectations, I regret that I wasn't capable of being the perfect partner."

If one sees a marital therapist at this time, then a fourth disappointment will emerge. No counselor is capable of being a miracle worker at a time like this. The disillusionment must be faced, owned, accepted and integrated. It is a sign of growth, not of disintegration, an evidence of maturing beyond the Dream. Disillusionment is both necessary and inevitable, if the two are to move beyond the mutually interlocking fantasies of romance to embrace the reality of being human together.

Disillusionment as Failing the Dream

When one has grown up worshipping the Dream—marital, vocational, economic—Dream, then its demise is a time of intense grieving, of confused mourning and of searching for its recovery. The disillusionment stage signals that someone or something has somehow failed.

The Dream may fail us or we may fail the Dream in several ways.

First, we may stifle the Dream. It may fail to be born. If the child is barred from dreaming, its hopes are dashed by the lack of esteem, the absence of support and confidence. Taught to think little of themselves, they either drift dreamlessly or too readily join another person— parent, spouse, employer, guru—in their dreams. In the time of disillusionment, one may discover that a dream needs to be released, redefined and transformed into realistic goals.

Second, we may abort a dream that is near birth because it is confusing or frightening or the cost is inflated by the demands of parents or family. So the future is sold out prematurely and the person settles for whatever comes along. Disillusionment with this sell-out may nudge us to reconceive the Dream and carry it to full term in responsible commitment.

Third, we may fail the Dream. By refusing to invest the effort needed to realize the Dream, we may let it die;

by not allowing the Dream to be tested with others we may harbor it within, but never risk attempting to fulfill it. The illusion within may be far from the reality without. One may dream of being a musician, but risk neither the training nor the practice. Disillusionment may call us to let go and embrace what is possible or to commit ourselves to the pursuit of what is desirable.

Fourth, we may idolize the Dream. Overcommitment to any goal allows it to become tyrannical, to rule one's life. Since the Dream is an expression of only a part of my self, then the triumph of one part over others may lead to neglect of the most important or the loss of the central values of one's life. Career may usurp integrity. Vocation may destroy marriage. Success may lead to sacrifice of family life or alienation from one's children.[8]

Most frequently, disillusionment calls us to see when we have sacrificed the more important for the less valuable and to restructure our lives by realigning our priorities. It is easy to sacrifice the long term to gain the short term; to forgo marital or familial intimacy in order to gain financial security; to fail on what is central to life in order to succeed in what is optional.

"I can always find another wife, but where could I get another job like this?" a counselee once asked me. One dream is eclipsing another, the moon is covering the sun, the lesser blacking out the more crucial and central.

Disillusionment is a time of review, of reflection, of reevaluation of commitments and dreams; a time for giving up what was attractive but not essential. As one approaches mid-life, the acceptance of limits, the narrowing of goals, the focusing of life values becomes increasingly important. One must give up the important, go beyond the necessary and discover the ultimate, if one is to live well. Disillusionment with past values and discovery of what is central in marriage and in life are two necessary steps toward maturity. Out of struggle comes awareness, out of frustration comes motivation, out of pain comes growth.

The third marriage within a marriage emerges as a couple moves from disillusionment with goals that have failed them to the discovery of what really matters.

Discovery

> Nothing has changed between us, we still have problems, but everything feels different. It's like the Dream is gone, but it doesn't matter. In fact, the things we really want—all dreams aside—we still have.

The Dream—you can be all I desire, I must be all that you admire—is eventually overtaken by disillusionment. Despair, distance and/or divorce may follow. Or we may break through to discovery.

The Dream fails, we discover the reality which endures. The other person may not match the ideal which I've carried deep within, yet the real may be a greater challenge, a more fulfilling complement, a more appropriate invitation to growth. Discarding the picture and embracing the person is like discarding the menu and enjoying the meal. Discovering the reality of the other is an adventure of many dimensions. As one discovers the real mate, one discovers new reality about and within the self, the other and the marriage. As the mate is encountered as the person she or he is, the meeting of two persons center to center bids each to grow. Authentic intimacy cannot occur in the meeting of dreams, but in the contact of real people; not from the sharing of masks, but from face touching face.

The Dream fails, we discover the reverse is what we needed all along. He wanted her to mother him, yet he resented mothering and her resemblance to his mother. As the dream-needs die, he discovers that what they both need is the freedom to be children with each other.

Her need to be invulnerable and securely in control has interlocked with his dream of being accepted and protected. Only when she neither seeks to control or be controlled, and he risks rejection do the two begin to discover intimacy. As the Dream is reversed, they discover each other.

He dreams of success at any price; he needs to drop out of the race and be available to his wife and kids. She dreams of finding her identity in her husband's success; she needs to plunge into life for herself and find her true self. In the failure of the Dream and in the disillusionment that follows, discovery breaks.

This third marriage is frequently more brief. Disillusionment breaks, and the discovery of what bonds, attracts and fulfills presses the couple toward the fourth marriage of depth. Yet for many couples, that third marriage may last for almost a decade.

The 40s are often a time of periods of discovery that arouse hope, followed by a slip back into disillusionment and discouragement. Then another strand of discovery breaks through until, sinew by sinew, the relationship is rediscovered. Commuting between marriages is not only inevitable during this period, it is necessary to complete the agenda that has accumulated during the disillusionment period. No person or couple has the energy to deal with more than a few parts of this at one time, but over time the marriage is rediscovered and re-experienced in depth.

Depth

> We're so much more close now, after 25 years
> of marriage, than we were the first 25 days.
> True, we have a different kind of closeness.
> The fire of passion is changed into a steady
> warmth that has permeated all of our life
> together.

The fourth marriage within a marriage is characterized by depth. Confident in their relationship, a couple is free to reveal increasingly deep feelings, values and self-understandings. Secure in each other's acceptance, they can express the fears that have been buried, the loneliness that was hidden, the wishes that were previously over-looked.

Intimacy deepens as both closeness and distance are guaranteed. Union is more rich as separation is insured. Separateness is not swallowed up in the union. Such security emerges only as the relationship has been tested, pushed to its limits of bonding through the disillusionment, revitalized in discovery and then set free to deepen at its own pace.

The depth characteristics are well described by the language Abraham Maslow and Carl Rogers have used to define the higher reaches of maturity. Such persons experience six signs of depth in life and relationship.

First, they experience life vividly "with full concentration and total absorption." The stage of depth invites people to live in the here and now. They enjoy the present moments of life fully, not as a means toward future ends, but as ends in themselves. Their lives are not perpetual preparation for the future; they are celebrated now. They are not awaiting what will be; they are embracing what is.

Second, they are each aware of the real inner self. Their openness to what is going on inside themselves has increased through the pain of the second stage of their marriage—disillusionment—and the breakthrough of the third—discovery. Now their own thoughts, feelings and states of being have become precious to them. Their self-images accurately reflect their real selves, so self-deception is minimal, self-defensiveness is rarely necessary. They resort to few myths about themselves and their individual or marital life. Having identified their defenses, they have given up most of them.

Third, they each take full responsibility for themselves and their choices. The needs to find themselves either by conforming to social expectations or by rebelling against them are largely past. They can choose to conform or refuse to conform, depending on the situation, on their values, and on their shared preferences. Yielding to or resisting social norms is not important in itself; what matters is fulfilling their own ethical and aesthetic values. These form slowly from growth within each and between them both.

Fourth, they have a positive, constructive attitude toward people beyond their marriage relationship. Having made peace with their extended families and having claimed full adulthood with their parents and siblings, they are at home in their broader network of relationships. They care, and this caring expresses both their ethical commitment and their sense of calling to serve and be useful.

Fifth, they risk change, choice and growth. The fear of the unknown is a lure rather than a barrier. Growth lies beyond our feelings of anxiety, and we move toward new self-other actualization by moving through the fear, not away from it. So they become increasingly comfortable with ambiguity, with disorder and indefiniteness, with doubt and uncertainty. They don't need guaranteed consistency. They can accept questions without answers. The contents of life do not need to be organized and labeled with each put in its place. Even confusion is accepted for what it is—the normal emotional condition of personal transformation and creative change.

Sixth, they have become distinctive and creative in living. This creativity is not necessarily focused on the role or work that they now choose—like dropping out of routine life to become an artist or author—but they are creative in innovative ways in all that they do. Their own sense of style spreads freshness throughout their life together and permeates their individual tasks. What they have chosen to do in life, they do well because they now do it with joy. They venture, they risk, they experiment in ways that enhance fulfillment and blend work and play.

As each develops a more firm center in herself and himself, both are able to experience greater depth in their closeness. The Dream has been transformed into depth.

EXERCISE 3: IDENTIFYING GOALS_____

Instructions. To explore what marriage can become and will be like when fully mature, set aside an hour to explore the central goals of a relationship with depth.

The following exercise lists the "depth characteristics" in the left column and the questions for exploration in the right column.

Sit comfortably—preferably facing each other so that

your knees touch—and then work through the questions one by one giving each other equal time to address each. Do not simply answer, use them as a basis to explore aspects of your relationship that can be deepened now.

The goals—being fully alive, aware, responsible, connected, changing and playfully creative—take many different forms from person to person within a marriage as well as from couple to couple. There are no right answers to this exercise, but you can be answering each other rightly as you become an answer to each other's growth and fulfillment.

Depth Characteristics

Questions for Discussion

Life is intense, vivid, meaningful. Each moment is an end in itself, not a means to an end.

Do we spend more time reliving the past or worrying about the future than celebrating the present?

Self-awareness has deepened. Their self-images reflect their real selves.

Is my self-image congruent with my real self? Is my image of our relationship an accurate reflection of who we are to each other?

Responsibility for themselves and their choices has set them free from either conforming to or resisting expectations.

Are we free to choose what we want without fear of rejection? Are we free to refuse what we do not want without feeling guilt?

Constructive attitudes toward people beyond their marriage, parents, family and network.

Are we concerned positively with our parents, siblings, friends, neighbors? Are we reconciled with those who have differences with us?

Change is welcomed; growth is valued; fear is an invitation to discover, risk, mature; ambiguity is accepted as part of all relationships.

Do we welcome change without defensiveness? Do we accept each other's growth without threat or resistance?

Creativity, innovation, play enrich their lives, their love, their work.

Can we play together freely? Are we creative in our work, our relaxation, our service for others?

4

COMMUNICATION

COMMUNICATION:

EXPECTATION

We communicate
out of
expectations
of what is
meant,
needed,
wanted,
owed,
required
to get
what
we
need.

MANIPULATION

We manipulate
out of frustration
by
persuading,
seducing,
coercing,
evading,
avoiding
to get
what
we
want.

INVITATION

We discover
that true
communication
is invitation.
We give up
manipulation,
we listen,
we invite,
we draw out
each other.

DIALOGUE

We dialogue
in
two-way,
equal,
mutual,
reciprocal,
conversational
exchange.

EXCUSE FEELINGS

We are
afraid of,
confused by,
embarrassed with,
cautious in
feeling our
feelings.

EXPLODE FEELINGS

We risk
sharing,
but find
feelings
uncontrolled,
unfocused,
confusing,
exploding.

EXPRESS FEELINGS

We own
and express,
appreciate
and
explore
each other's
feelings.

EXPERIENCE FEELINGS

We are
free to
follow
with
both
feelings
and
thoughts.

Lisa

"I just can't take anymore. His indifference is killing me. I'd like to work things out, but he won't listen when I talk, and he won't talk when there is a problem we need to discuss. We end up fighting over nothing, almost every night. He just keeps telling me to get off his back.

"Last night I was telling him about the plans for our son's birthday party this Friday night. He agreed to it last week, but now he says he's going to the lake for the weekend, fishing. All the invitations have been sent out, and I can't do the whole thing alone. I ended up screaming at him and he was just staring into his drink.

"This is so different from the first 13 years of our marriage. Any complaints I had I just kept to myself, but I get stomach pains and I can't sleep when I keep it all inside. I have to talk, but what's the use when he won't listen or give me any response except a deaf ear."

Larry

"I don't see why we have to fight all the time. I get so tired of Lisa's getting on me for everything. She is always after me. It's like being in the army, or worse, like being at home with my mother. She plans everything the way she wants it, then maneuvers me to fit into her plans.

"Like Jim's birthday party. She says she checked it out with me. I don't remember her mentioning anything. Besides his birthday isn't until Sunday. We could have it Sunday night after my fishing trip. I'll pick up the pizza for the gang and save her all the work she would put into the Friday night bash after the game.

"We got along just great until the last two years. All this talk about sharing feelings leaves me cold. Sure I have feelings too, but what has that got to do with talking all the time. Well I've said enough. Probably too much."

We just don't communicate anymore," a couple in their third year of marriage complains.

No marriage begins with perfect communication, and theirs was no exception. The blending of selves which takes place in the early bonding of lovers had given them the illusion of complete understanding or at least that both of them were being understanding of each other. Now the connections are failing them.

"I thought he cared about my needs and feelings, now I'm not so sure."

Love is expressed unmistakably with the eyes. In giving attention, we give affection. In early marriage the attention may be largely motivated by attraction and passion. As the couple matures, loving presence may emerge. It must if the relationship is to go forward.

"I thought she understood how I feel. She used to listen to me. Now all she does is complain."

Love is expressed undeniably with the ears. In hearing another's true intentions, we give affection. In respecting intentions as the other's central motivations, in spite of puzzling or confusing feelings expressed and behaviors exhibited, we give love.

"I thought he would be there when I needed him, but now he's not home when he is home."

Love is expressed unequivocally in the time scheduled and the availability offered. The assurance that each will be there for the other when needed, when expected, when desired is the confidence of being loved.

A relationship is as good as its communication is clear.

A marriage is as strong as its communication is honest.

A family is as healthy as its communication is open.

Communication patterns evolve dramatically throughout the course of a marriage. To early marriage we bring a rich legacy of expectations that color virtually all understandings exchanged. As the second marriage begins, both find themselves resorting to manipulation. As this becomes exhausted, communication can mature to invitation and eventually to authentic dialogue.

Communication is the nervous system of a marriage. The communication pathways in a relationship carry the messages of life, love and vitality from one part of that third body—the one flesh of marriage relationship—to another. Clear, open, honest communication creates a warm and vital relationship by transmitting energy, integrity and intimacy from one person to another.

The style of communication, its level of honesty, openness and directness are among the most revealing signs of health in a marriage. The marriage is no better than the communication. In order to decipher what is going on between two people, we look first at the way they communicate. To diagnose the health or unhealth of the marriage, we examine how the two express their thoughts and feelings, their wants and needs to each other.

When couples talk of a lack of communication, they may simply not talk about anything of importance. They talk, but not about what matters. They both may be so wrapped up in their own agendas that neither can hear what the partner is saying. Sometimes it's the silent treatment; at other times it's empty words. Or the lack may be in the inability to gain real attention; one feels turned off or tuned out. Most often, the inability to communicate is measured by the difficulty in getting what one wants from the other, of hearing what one wants to hear from the partner.

Communication is a meeting of meaning. It happens when my meaning meets your meaning across the bridge of words and we meet. When the intent in the speaker and the impact on the listener match, then communication has

LACK OF COMMUNICATION

If you are not expecting open communication, explore what is lacking by discussing each item and comparing ratings given to each.

1 = strongly agree, 2 = somewhat agree, 3 = neutral,
4-somewhat disagree, 5 = strongly disagree

HE   **SHE**

1

1 2 3 4 5   Our lack of communication is that we   1 2 3 4 5
              simply do not talk about feelings or
              issues.

2

1 2 3 4 5   Our lack of communication is that I do   1 2 3 4 5
              not understand what my partner is
              trying to say.

3

1 2 3 4 5   Our lack of communication is that one   1 2 3 4 5
              of us talks and the other refuses to
              reciprocate—the silent treatment.

4

1 2 3 4 5   Our lack of communication is that I   1 2 3 4 5
              don't hear what I want to hear from my
              partner.

5

1 2 3 4 5   Our lack of communication is that my   1 2 3 4 5
              partner tunes me out, at least I do not
              feel heard.

Figure 1

taken place. In marriage, the meanings of each person run deep, two or three generations deep. The meanings are colored by the expectations of past, present and future.

Communication Is Expectation

"Why do I need to tell him? He would know what I need, what I'm feeling, if he loved me."

Expectations—the subtle demands that shape what we see, hear and speak—spring nimbly from generation to generation. What we do not inherit, we create from our own developmental process from childhood to adulthood. To add a third layer, we construct interlocking expectations from our own bonding and early love relationship. This three-tier mass may serve to determine virtually all that is communicated in the first stages of marriage.

Expectations from the Familial Past

Two families merge in marriage, not just two persons. Although modern individualism pretends otherwise, parents, grandparents and sometimes great grandparents may be present in a couple's communication. A marital conflict may not be between the two combatants at all; the parents may be speaking through them with their old anger still reacting to the grandparent's rage.

In a profound sense, expectations, like much else in life, never begin; they continue from generation to generation of humans who carry their culture forward in obedience. The instructions of the past, like those of a hypnotist are obeyed faithfully.

"In the family situation," British psychiatrist R.D. Laing writes, "the hypnotists (parents) are already hypnotized (by their parents) and are carrying out their instructions, by bringing their children up to bring their children up, in such a way that includes not realizing that one is carrying out instructions: since one instruction is not to think that one is thus instructed."[1]

This process of "mapping the past onto the future," as Laing describes expectations, is so well concealed that it is immediately denied if it does come to light. If any one in a family begins to recognize that the parents are puppets controlled by the strings of expectations from grandparents and that he or she is only the shadow of a puppet, with whom can this be discussed? Who will understand? Certainly not the family system since a part of the hypnotic instruction is often "you will not notice that you are carrying out instructions. This is the way things are, as they should and must be." But when one partner's instructions clash with another's expectations, as they invariably do, a tangled mass emerges.

"The majority of adults (including myself) are or have been, more or less, in a post-hypnotic trance, induced in early infancy: we remain in this state until—when we dead awaken, we shall find that we have never lived."[2]   My great-grandfather was a Mennonite bishop who ordered his life around the expectations of the churches he served. He lived by the demands of his people, and they lived by his. My grandfather, a minister serving under his father never said no to the patriarch. My mother who cared for them both emotionally, physically and spiritually carried their expectations forward to the next generation.

I, like three older brothers, entered the ministry with deep commitment to be available others and with intense loyalty to the church. The persistent expectations of past generations may repeat themselves with positive power as well as with negative binding. Often there are both. Some patterns are replicated virtually unretouched; others reverse themselves, mirror images of reaction. Is it any surprise then that a major conflict in my life has been over fulfilling or resisting the expectations of the church, over claiming the freedom to serve out of love rather than duty?

We are, each of us, a whole community of people who live on within us. Family, neighbors, friends, mentors, heroes, villains. Their models, their values, their fears, their hopes, their instructions, their expectations are present now within us. When we talk to each other, the multiple voices speak from our depths.

Every marriage is a union of two families, two communities of experience that collide at the outset and compete long-term. In no marriages does this not occur; only the degree of union varies. In highly fused relationships, each partner is more controlled by past familial expectations than by present marital understandings. The more free persons are, the more they are enriched by their past, not enchained by it.

I am not my past, I am heir to it and its blend of riches and obligations. I am open to my past, but not dominated by it; I am instructed by my heritage, but not controlled by it. These are truthful affirmations, as far as I am aware, but there are expectations beneath awareness. Early learnings are alive and well in my unconscious. Family patterns are powerful and functional in my inner world of feelings and thoughts.

I communicate out of expectations past, I communicate with expectations present.

Expectations from My Personal Past

"I started life as a child," Bill Cosby noted. So did we all.

And the story of development is the story of unfolding, interlocking expectations. These expectations—

consistent and contradictory, enabling and entrapping—
were assimilated from the first peek-a-boo games:

*(I expect the parent to reappear and end my abandon-
ment)* through the shame and guilt of training

(I will be found out, shamed and punished, if I disobey)
to the internalized expectations of school age

(I must be good at school work or I will be rejected) and
youth

*(I will be accepted only when I comply, because I per-
form, if I am attractive enough).*

That our individual collections of expectations are
unique is such an obvious, even redundant, statement, yet
it must be noted that—in this respect—no two children
have the same parents, go to the same school, belong to
the same peer group. We each filter, organize and remember life experiences in ways that protect us from repeating
what was painful or permit us to regain what was satisfying.

We each develop layer on layer of expectations
throughout the stages of life development. The primal
expectations of trust or mistrust are expanded into the
basic emotions of anger, shame, fear, guilt, sadness, joy,
pride, confidence and stubbornness in our second and
third years. The expectations take on color and power as
they are energized by feelings, those energies with which
we experience our perceptions.

The budding of conscience and the formation of an ego
ideal signal the internalization of moral expectations, followed by the imposition of educational expectations from
teachers and peers. Adolescence erupts, and with it layer
on layer of expectations—sexual, moral, ideological, relational, vocational and so on—which must be knit into a
coherent sense of identity and personhood. All these layers combine to form the sense of selfhood one brings to

LAYERS OF EXPECTATION

5. **PERSONHOOD EXPECTATIONS**
Interpersonal expectations
from peers, family, community:
"I can choose who I am."
"I can risk openness with others."
"I can trust my mentors/models."
"I can claim my values."

4. **EDUCATIONAL EXPECTATIONS**
Performance
expectations
before others:
"I must produce to have worth."
"I can be capable/competent."
"I am incompetent, so what?"
"I am what I can do."

6. **COMMUNAL EXPECTATIONS**
Relational expectations
Marital expectations
Parental expectations
Career expectations
Communal expectations

3. **FAMILIAL EXPECTATIONS** (5-6)
Moral expectations
from parents/siblings:
"I must be good or else."
"I can be bad and get by."
"I am always on trial."
"I will usurp father/mother."

7. **VOCATIONAL EXPECTATIONS**
Creative and recreative
expectations in life vocation:
Recreate marriage
Reassess career
Readjust parenting
Rediscover goals.

2. **INFANT EXPECTATIONS** (3-4)
Emotional
expectations
from the trust
of self and parents:
"I will be good to earn love."
"I will be bad to be noticed."
"I will not risk exposure."
"I will not exert my will."
"I will always feel shame."

8. **INTEGRITY EXPECTATIONS**
Integrative expectations
of life review and celebration:
Disengage from work
Discover wisdom
Adapt in change
Be reconciled to death.

1. **PRIMAL EXPECTATIONS** (1-2)
Intuitive expectations
formed from the
trust of the
mothering other:
"I will never trust again."
"I will always be on guard."
"I will trust those who love me."
"I will always be helpless/hopeless."

Figure 2

marriage, to career, to parenthood, to life in the community of faith as well as the other communities one joins.

In each of these stages, shown in figure 2, are four basic dangers. I may over-expect (inflated expectations), under-expect (absence of positive expectations), mis-expect (learn or choose false expectations), fail what I expect (fail the expectations which are central to my life).

Honoring the expectations which guide my identity and reevaluating the expectations which are unrealistic are ongoing tasks throughout life. They become the central agenda in early marriage, and we never outgrow the need to reconsider and redirect the expectations we bring to this most challenging of all relationships.

Expectations from the Marital Present

My expectations may be rooted in the past, but they are being formed and reformed now from the plots and counterplots of our marital drama. I not only map the past onto the future, I am drawing maps now, maps of expectations.

I have hunches about what my partner thinks and feels. These may help me intuit what the other is experiencing. But if I trust the hunch more than the other's words, I hear and see only my hunch. These hunches express the images which trigger my thoughts and feelings, images that make up complex pictures.

I have pictures of my partner in my head. These combine past scenes of our life together with present scenarios of our relationship style. We need pictures of each other in our heads in order to make sense out of our communication. But a picture is a temporary representation that serves to make sense out of the fragments of information I receive in each conversational exchange. Each of us must supply a major part of the picture in each transaction; we fill in the gaps with expectations based in part on past experiences of each other and, in even larger part, on our fears and hopes.

These pictures serve us as long as we use them to make meaningful patterns out of each other's words, then we redraw them by the next response. The most useful pictures are penciled in, easily erased, corrected, adjusted to the new data of each conversation. Partners who draw indelible portraits of each other hold unchangeable expectations. They prefer the picture to the reality, as did the mother who, when complimented on her beautiful baby, replied, "Oh, he's nothing, you ought to see his picture."

The more aware I am of my pictures—of how I see you—the more intentional I can be about correcting my misperceptions, of destroying outdated pictures, of choosing to see you, not my representation of you.

From the raw material of hunches, images, and pictures, we draw maps—patterns of expectations—of a partner's emotional landscape. These marital maps are added to the collected maps of my parents and siblings as well as those of admired models or despised villains from my childhood and young adulthood. No one's emotional filing system is perfect and, in times of frustration, we call up the wrong maps, take similarities in one part as typical of the whole or react to one map as though it were another. Small wonder we get confused when negotiating differences, since in stress all humans regress. The more stressed, the more we become aware of how distressingly similar the present person is to a past figure in our development. He's "just like" my mother/father, she says; she's "just like" my father/mother, he concludes. The small part that resembles is taken to represent the whole which is quite different.

This mutual cross—mapping, which clinicians call a bilateral transference, usually lasts from 7 to 10 years.

The exchange of expectations may be so well matched that communication flows easily and with little distortion. If two middle children marry, particularly if each had a sibling of the opposite sex, then mutual horizontal conversation may come readily. But when an eldest marries a youngest or two only children marry or a brother of brothers marries a sister of sisters, then expectations will be nonsymmetrical and conflictual. When maps don't match at all and few expectations overlap, then every communication attempt is like inventing the wheel all over again.

What makes this period so difficult is the inability of one or both to call expectations by their proper name. Instead, the expectations one lays on another are called rights or responsibilities or obligations or moral imperatives or evidences that "you love me." Often they are considered the only reality, the inevitable and unavoidable way to be mature, sensible or responsible.

Not everything is relative, a matter of taste, but much of what makes up a marriage is just that, much more than most are willing to recognize in the first decade of living with each other. Relaxing our demands, giving up inherited definitions, welcoming the freedom of negotiation and conciliation are all signs of growth.

When we communicate out of expectations of what is meant, needed, wanted, owed, required but do not work through to agreement, we pass each other by. Feelings get buried, and when they do break out they are confused and conflicted. We are afraid of our feelings because they are rarely congruent with our expectations. And when they well up, they warn us of expectations unfulfilled by the partner or of expectations imposed upon us that we resent. So feelings are best overlooked, we think; emotions are to be held in check and hid in silence unless they are totally acceptable responses.

The 20s are years of fulfilled and unfulfilled expectations but, as first marriages are, a time for smiling—
expectantly—and getting on. Unfortunately, expectation
leads to manipulation. They are two sides to the same coin
of controlling communications. Plant an expectation, reap
manipulation.

Communication as Manipulation

"Why are you always asking questions? Why don't you say
what you want? Don't you know I hate questions? Don't
you think I had enough of that in my home? Why should I
put up with it now?"

Manipulation—the ever-present temptation when
communication falters—characterizes the second marriage within a marriage. As the early expectations are
being frustrated, either or both persons tend to fall back
on the games, strategies and dances which they observed
in their family of origin. Often the behaviors appear which
they disliked most. As what is hated in one's past is replicated, the anger or disgust is turned outward on the other
person.

"If you weren't acting like this, obviously I wouldn't be
driven to such lengths. All I want is open communication
but you keep trying to control me."

Or the person may turn against the self and accept
blame for all that is going wrong between them. As the
intolerable increases, the internal conflict intensifies.

"Why do I keep ruining things between us? Somehow I
always bring out the worst in my partners?"

Manipulative models are present in most of our lives,
and negative models, because of the anxiety they arouse,
seem to stick like burrs in the folds of our memory and

Persuasive Communication in Marriage

Three basic attitudes in persuasive communication shape a relationship.

RAPE—Coercion in Marriage

The intention is to achieve agreement by whatever means is necessary: punishment or reward, intimidation or coercion, violence or violation are all options.

The attitude is one-way. The other partner is seen as an inferior object to be manipulated or used.

The consequences are the silencing or destruction of the other.

SEDUCTION—Control in Marriage

The intention is to achieve agreement through charm or deceit: any strategy for outsmarting, outmaneuvering, outwitting the other.

The attitude is one-way. Indifferent to the identity and integrity of the other, the seductive persuader has no respect for the other's freedom to choose.

The consequences are destructive: the most distinctively human ability—the right to choose with understanding is being limited or denied.

LOVE—Mutuality in Marriage

The intention is to reach agreement by mutual exploration of the issue. The lover wants equality of power, a mutually satisfactory relationship.

The attitude is two-way. The lover views the other as an equal partner in dialogue, as a person to be respected and prized.

The consequences are creative bonding. Free assent to all concerns is invited, open statement of positions and full respect for each other's agreement or disagreement are assured.[3]

Figure 3

reappear at disconcerting times. As the passage from early marriage to middle marriage begins, the frustrated, denied, exhausted expectations turn coercive and covert manipulations multiply. Communication becomes more complex. Messages are multilevel. Feelings, concealed as dangerous and excused as inappropriate, now begin to explode. They emerge in unfocused and uncontrolled ventilation.

Communication, when focused on persuasion, takes three basic forms. These have been characterized as rape, seduction and love. The first is raw coercion, the second manipulation, the third is mutuality. The three forms, shown in figure 3, are basic communication styles, but the metaphor can be expanded to include other styles such as infatuation, romance or prostitution.

In marital stress, people who previously communicated effectively as lovers, find themselves being coercive or seductive. Whenever the goal is a win-lose victory, violation of the other's personhood is inevitable. Of course one can be a lover in intent, but a seducer or even a rapist in style. For those who believe that the end justifies the means, the intent is invariably virtuous, but the means may be less so.

Coercion in marriage is not an acceptable solution in any conflict, nor is it a tolerable style of communication. But the number of ways couples communicate coercively is astounding.

Manipulation in marriage is not an appropriate communication or relationship behavior, but the forms of manipulation are as common to most couples as their combs or toothbrushes. Such strategies are: using questions rather than risking statements, ignoring the other's point while pressing one's own, withholding information then suddenly unmasking the concealed, misquoting

THE ART OF MANIPULATION

Dirty fighting strategies for getting your own way

STRATEGY

1. **Timing**   Catch them off guard rather than choose a good time.

2. **Turf**   Pick your best turf rather than choose a neutral place.

3. **Anxiety**   Step up the anxiety rather than set a caring atmosphere.

4. **Fogging**   Filibuster, fog and fume instead of communicating equally.

5. **Mystifying**   Ramble, chain react, confuse rather than be clear and honest.

6. **Generalizing** Universalize and exaggerate instead of simplify and focus.

7. **Analyze**   Intellectualize, theorize, advise instead of admitting pain.

8. **Gunnysacking** Save up grievances rather than deal with here and now.

9. **Neutrality**   Be silent, superior, detached rather than open and present.

10.	Temper	Hide anger then ventilate rage rather than clean anger.
11.	Blaming	Find who is at fault rather than practice no-fault fights.
12.	Righteousness	Find who is right instead of find what's right.
13.	Exit	Walk out, clam up, shut off instead of working through.
14.	Questioning	Use clever or concealed questions instead of statements.
15.	Triangling	Pit people against people instead of dealing firsthand.
16.	Put-downs	Use sarcasm, jibes, digs rather than share humor.
17.	Undermining	Undermine self-esteem rather than enrich self-respect.
18.	Guilt	Play either judge or martyr to hook guilt not responsibility.
19.	Mind reading	Read or rape the other's mind rather than listen, wait, learn.
20.	Delaying	Ignore, forget, postpone rather than honor commitments.[5]

Figure 4

sources or using critical quotes from people not present, pitting people against people and so on and on. The partial listing of common strategies in figure 4 may miss your favorite means of manipulating in an intimate relationship—if any can be termed favorite. Most of us hate all these strategies when on the receiving end, but excuse them as necessary when giving them. Perhaps it is "more blessed to give than to receive."[4]

Out of frustration, we manipulate by persuading, seducing, coercing, evading, avoiding to get what we want from each other. But such strategies are self-destructive. The means whereby defeats the end goal.

The basic rules of manipulative behavior are:

Manipulators get manipulated. Those who seek to manipulate others are manipulated in turn, not just by their own strategies, but by the enmeshed interlocking relationships they form as their means of manipulating. One who seeks to manipulate the partner is manipulated by the partner. Full circle. What goes around comes around.

Controllers get controlled. Those who seek to control others lose control and are controlled, whether they recognize it or not. In marriage, the controlling spouse may appear to have all the power, but the submissive one may win more often through passivity, martyrdom, guilt. One cannot *not* be powerful. There are differentials of power and different kinds of power but none who is truly powerless in a relationship. Full circle. One reaps what one sows. One gets what one gives.

It is no surprise that many marriages end in the passage into this marriage-within-a marriage or that they bottom out, exhausted by the attempts to control, shape, manipulate, remake each other. The more frustrated the partners become with their inability to reform the other, the more intense the cycles of pressuring and persuading become.

"We simply can't communicate," they conclude. They can and do communicate, of course, but not positively and productively. In fact, they cannot stop communicating. We cannot not communicate. There is no opposite to the word "communicate," just as there is no antonym for the word "behavior"—we go on communicating, but in alienating rather than affiliating ways.

Love needs to be set free from the overlay of expectations and pried loose from the many layers of demands that lie beneath. The covenant given in figure 5 has provided a basis for many couples to test out their practice of loving relationship.

Sit, facing the person you love—either in reality or with an empty chair if you rehearse it alone—and read each paragraph aloud. Then paraphrase it in your own words, changing those parts which do not feel right to you.

The first paragraph affirms the worth of oneself, the equal preciousness of the other. Any Western narcissistic individualist can read the first half confidently, but the second half requires a self-giving movement of authentic love. How would you change it?

The second paragraph defines the self and sets boundaries around personhood. It equally respects the boundaries and selfhood of the other. It balances mutual responsibility *with* the other while refusing to play god by being responsible for or to idolize the other by being responsible to another.

The third paragraph owns anger, resentment and hurt (the emotions which surround demands) and then recognizes that our angry demands express our expectations. These godlike expectations need to be canceled before love becomes unconditional. When one is free to have no

LOVE AND EXPECTATIONS
A Covenant

I am I. I do love me.
My privilege to be me,
My opportunity to do my thing,
My right to become my real self
Are infinitely precious to me.
You are you. I equally love you.
Your privilege to be you,
Your opportunity to do your thing,
Your right to be your true self
Are equally precious to me.

I own my experience of me,
The thoughts I think,
The emotions I feel,
The words I speak,
The choices I make,
The beliefs I hold,
The actions I take are mine.
For them I am fully responsible.
Your thoughts, emotions, words,
Choices, beliefs, actions are yours.
For them I am in no way
responsible.
I will be responsible with you,
but not for you or to you.

You are you.
Inside any anger or hurt
Which I feel in our relationship
Is my demand that you change
And live as I prescribe.
You are not in this world
To live up to my expectations.
Nor do I exist to fulfill yours.
I will have no demands
As conditions for loving you,
Although many demands
For living with you.
On these I will seek solutions
Satisfying to us both.

I am I and you are you.
If, in being our true selves,
We find each other in equal regard,
It's beautiful. If not, it's sad.
Such finding can only come
As you love me for being me
And I love you for being you.
I will do all I can to find you.
I willingly accept
Whatever responsibility is mine
For loving, seeking and finding.
For when, simultaneously,
We each fully affirm the other
As he is, as she is,
We meet, and we are we.

Figure 5

conditions for living, but many conditions for living that can be mutually negotiated, then both can reach satisfactory solutions.

The final paragraph is a pledge to seek an equal, mutual, lasting relationship. Yet it recognizes that such mutual love cannot be forced; it is a gift. It cannot be manipulated; it begins when manipulation ends and invitations are exchanged.

How have you paraphrased your covenant? What do you discover in comparing your words with these?

Communication as Invitation

"Why don't you say what you're feeling? Oh, let me say that another way. What I really want is to know how you feel about me right now. When you're ready to talk, I'm ready to listen."

The most powerful form of communication is not the question, nor the argumentative proposition, nor the blaming accusation; the most effective and potent communication is the invitation. The most useful statements in any relationship begin with "Tell me about your day" or "I'd like to hear how you're feeling about . . . . "

Invitations are open-ended since they do not lead, trap, command or ambush the other like closed questions that must be answered in the way the questioner is pressing.

Invitations are freeing, rather than controlling. They respect the other's timing, interest and direction. They welcome sharing without limiting what will be shared. The two contrasting columns in figure 6 highlight the differences between closed and open communication styles. This is not simply two different ways of expressing things,

CLOSED AND OPEN COMMUNICATION STYLES

QUESTIONS	INVITATIONS

THE LEADING QUESTION limits or restricts the possible responses of the other.

> "Don't you think that . . . ?"
> "Isn't it true that you . . . ?"
> "Wouldn't you rather . . . ?"

THE OPEN INVITATION is an open-ended request for the other to communicate,

> "Tell me about . . . . "
> "I like to hear about . . . "

THE PUNITIVE QUESTION seeks to expose the other's wrongness, belittles the other's intelligence, judges the other's behavior.

> "Why did you say that?"
> "How could you think that . . . ?"

is nonpunitive,

It frees communication.

THE COMMAND QUESTION actually makes a demand or imposes a command while masquerading as a simple question.

> "When are you going to do something about . . . ?"
> "Why don't you get going on . . . ?"

is undemanding,

It welcomes communication.

THE SCREENED QUESTION conceals the intent of the communication by making a multilevel, multiple choice query.

> "What would you like . . . ?"
> "Why don't you choose this time?"
> "What do you mean by that?"

is single level,

It clarifies communication.

THE SET-UP QUESTION maneuvers the other into a vulnerable position ready for the ax.

> "Isn't it true that you . . . ?"
> "Didn't you once say that . . . ?"

is transparent.

It is caring communication.

Figure 6

rather it is two different ways of being with each other.

The questioning way of being is controlling, competitive, coercive. When, in each other's presence, one feels less free, less able to be oneself, less capable of expressing and disclosing oneself fully and without fear.

The invitational way of being with each other is spontaneous, nondefensive, open and free. It welcomes the other as an equal partner in dialogue, it calls out the best in the other, it bids the other to grow. Invitation facilitates self-disclosure since it reduces the threat of evaluation, judgment and rejection.

Invitation, above all, respects the other person's freedom to accept or refuse, to respond or to remain silent. It values the free response of love and prefers it above all else. Control, manipulation or obligation may all produce more immediate compliance, but co-munication, co-operation, co-laboration are not the results. When the relationship of the communicators matters even more than the content of the particular communication, then *how* one communicates may matter more than *what* one communicates. The classic research by Albert Mehrabian revealed that in relational communication, the impact on the other is far more nonverbal than verbal. Only 7 percent of what is communicated is in the actual content of the words, 28 percent is in tone of voice and 55 percent is in posture, facial expression and gestures. What we are speaks more clearly and persuasively than what we say.

His formula is:

Total impact = .07 verbal plus
　　　　　　　.28 vocal plus
　　　　　　　.55 facial.[6]

The basic rules of body language are: when the content of a communication conflicts with the tone of voice, one always believes the tone of voice; when two contrasting messages are given, it's the body that tells the truth; when the voice says yes and the face says no, the face wins.

Invitation is something you are as well as something you do. When couples communicate without imposing expectations or attempting manipulation, they are moving into their third marriage style. Often the invitational style is possible when anxiety is low, but under stress one or both will regress to manipulation. As this happens with less and less frequency, the third marriage of equality is arriving. The partners are no longer reacting to each other or their past history and agenda; they are responding to the other and focusing on the here and now (see fig. 7).

The responder speaks from a position of centeredness, of a clear "I." This "I-Position" requires both that persons know who they are and that they respect others for who they are. Recognizing the other person's right to his/her own thoughts, feelings and actions, the responder speaks for the self, not for the other, expressing concerns from the self, not quoting, mind reading, judging, analyzing as ways of speaking from the other's world of action and experience.

The responder has become an invitation to live, an invitation to love, an invitation to understanding. This third marriage within a marriage is durable; it will last for the long haul through the 40s and 50s until communication takes on that relaxed, mutual give-and-take of dialogue which is possible in depth only in the fourth marriage.

True many couples dialogue well in courtship. Engagement is often one of the healthiest periods because intimacy is pledged, individuality is still guaranteed by their singleness, and identity is still more crisply defined by youthful energy and hope. But the depth of dialogue is limited by the brief life experience. Early and middle mar-

RESPONDING AND REACTING

I POSITION

I am a *responder.*

I respond to the other's pain or joy freely, voluntarily, openly.

I can respond, saying,

"I am . . . . "
"I think . . . . "
"I feel . . . . "
"I want . . . . "

in clear "I messages."

I will be radically honest:

"I don't like what is now happening between us. I am willing to take this step to change it. I want to hear your response."

Each of us is sole owner of his or her feelings, choices and actions. So each is free to respond in love.

WE-YOU-THEY-IT POSITIONS

I am a *reactor.*

I react to the other's pain or joy automatically, emotionally, defensively.

I must react, saying,

"You make me feel . . . . "
"You make me do . . . . "
"You won't let me . . . . "
"You keep me from . . . . "

in blaming "you messages."

I have to be critically frank:

"You are driving me up a wall, you are making me very angry, you must change or you will ruin our relationship."

Each must feel for the other, hurt for the other, protect the other, so each must react in obligation.

Figure 7

riage have periods of dialogue, but these are complicated times for all couples. Authentic dialogue waits for our maturation as persons and partners into full adulthood.

Communication as Dialogue

"Conversation is a big part of our life. I enjoy the way she thinks, she seems to enjoy me. We aren't trying to compete with our ideas, but to complete an idea that we're exploring. I find I'm as interested in her point of view as I am in my own."

Dialogue is the goal of all loving communication, since love is the state in which another's safety and security is as important as one's own. Marital dialogue happens at many levels of intensity, across a wide spectrum of emotions.

Intimate dialogue occurs in the vulnerable self-disclosing of warmth and affection. The pleasure of communication comes equally from each sensing the pleasure in the partner as well as from the pleasure of the other's company. The joy of such dialogue is the enjoyment of being enjoyed.

Routine dialogue characterizes much of the interchange of living together. Each partner is concerned with both hearing and being heard. The intent of the speaker may not match the impact on the listener, but they possess the sensitivity to check it out, to clarify, to restate until both feel heard.

Conflictual dialogue is a joint struggle to alter either or both points of view. Dialogue goes directly and honestly to the difference between "me and thee." At its best, conflictual dialogue rejects ideas or behavior in the other while confirming the partner as a person. Dialogue shows how deeply important the other person is to you, how seriously you take both his/her point of view and personhood as a co-participant in life. It validates, confirms and affirms the other. This requires an immense toughness of self to contradict and conflict with as little defensiveness as possible.

For example, as anxiety rises in disagreement, one may be flooded by negative feelings. To express this by saying, "I am getting angry with you" is far different than saying, "I don't like you." The latter judges, excludes and rejects the partner in dialogue. It begins the ending of dialogue. But owning of anger is an authentic admission of feelings, and risks going deeper in the dialogue. Owning of anger reveals faith in the other and in the relationship; it shows trust that we can handle disagreement even when it is filled with lively emotions.

> The great test of a marriage is the ability of partners to listen to each other when in conflict. Can the one embrace the other when differences arise? Each is tested. "Do I have enough tolerance for myself to embrace a person whose very being I learn stimulates my awareness of those qualities I dislike in myself?"[7]

Dialogue is based on (a) self-confirmation, (b) trust in the relationship (c) confirmation of the other. Faith in oneself is required to be a trusting person, who trusts even an enemy or one's ability to go on listening and communicating even in the face of enmity. Trust in the relationship expresses the commitment to keep the communication open, equal, reciprocal in as far as this is possible. Confirmation of the other then follows naturally as one extends that trust in the confidence that we can understand each other, we can negotiate differences, we can reach a mutu-

Dialogue is to love
what blood is to the body;
when the flow of blood stops
the body dies.
When dialogue stops,
love dies and resentment and hate are born.
But dialogue can restore
a dead relationship.
Indeed this is the miracle
of dialogue: it can bring
relationship into being
and it can bring into being
a relationship that has died. [8]

> Dialogue goes directly and honestly
> to the difference between "me and thee,"
> and this requires an immense toughness of self
> —for it does combat without going on the defensive. [9]

No one can develop freely in this world
and find a full life
without feeling understood
by at least one person.
No one comes to know the self
through introspection
or in the solitude of a personal diary.
Rather it is in dialogue,
in meeting with other persons. [10]

> Relationship is dialogue.
> To whatever degree
> one part of the dialogue is lost,
> to that degree
> the relationship ceases to exist. [11]

ally satisfactory solution because you do act in good faith.

This dialogue has been described best by Martin Buber as an I-Thou relationship in which each becomes a single I of integrity and prizes the other as a Thou with inviolable dignity.

Communicating in dialogue takes years of maturing. It requires separate "single" identities. It depends on clearly formed understandings of each other's trustworthiness and constancy in calm or in conflict.

For a marriage to develop the depth necessary for such mutual self-disclosing and other embracing takes years. We begin working toward such dialogue in the earliest stages of relationship. We taste and enjoy it in our best moments of closeness, and gradually we gain the maturity to sustain it even in times of higher stress.

Dialogue is both a peak experience and a plateau that can be achieved with sustained depth as the relationship matures. The ability to maintain dialogue through disagreement is the mark of proven trust and tested commitment. Silence has come to mean confidence in each other, conversation has come to mean the meeting of meanings that are filled with promise and surprise.

EXERCISE 4: EXPERIENCING DIALOGUE___

Instructions. Each of us communicates according to the contracts we assume or have pledged with our partners in dialogue. Often these contracts are unverbalized and even unconscious. To finally express them to each other or to renegotiate and clarify old covenants that need to be brought up-to-date is helpful.

The covenant of equality and mutuality in dialogue that follows, offers seven clauses which pledge open, genuine and just communication. Couples have used it for an annual

Communication As Dialogue

I will claim my right to be equally heard. I am I. I want to be heart.	1 Equal Hearing	I will respect your right to be equally heard. You are you. I want to hear you.
I will claim my full ownership for my side of the dialogue. I will not let you speak for me.	2 Equal Ownership	I will respect your sole owner-ship for your side of the dialogue. I will not speak for you.
I will meet you now as the person you truly are. I will stop myself from speaking to my image of you. I cancel the demand that you be what you were or become what I want.	3 Equal Presence	I will be with you now as the person I truly am. I will not be try-ing to match or fulfill your image of me. I claim the freedom to change what I was and choose who I am becoming.
I will not mind read your thoughts nor choose my words out of my expectations of what I think you think. I will feel freely and speak frankly what I see, I think, I feel, I want.	4 Equal Integrity	I will not second-guess your wants nor anticipate your responses so as to limit your right nor inhibit your freedom to speak and choose what you see, think, feel, want.
I take full responsibility for how I see things and how I say things. I will neither blame you for my responses nor accept blame for yours. I am always responsible. I am never to blame.	5 Equal Responsibility	I honor your sole responsibility for how you see things and how you say things. I will accept no shaming for my responses nor shame you for yours. You are always accountable. You need never feel shame.
I will own my words and acts, see them as my choices, prize them as my responses, recognize where they are hurtful, modify them willingly to seek mutually satisfying relationship.	6 Equal Conciliation	I will admit my mistakes. I will not grovel to gain your approval, nor ask you to "apologize" to earn my acceptance. I will change my part in our two-person problem.
I want in no way to squander my freedom to be fully me when I am with you.	7 Equal Freedom	I want in no way to hamper your freedom to be wholly you when with me. [12]

checkup on communication. Facing each other, each reads a clause, then debriefs feelings and thoughts in agreement, in disagreement, in application to the relationship and in reflection on here-and-now experience.

A covenant provides a useful tool for testing your ability to dialogue in any stage of marriage. Experiment with the covenant provided to discover and sharpen your own and to deepen your experience of dialogue.

Sit facing each other.

One partner reads the first clause and then describes how it fits or does not fit your marriage experience.

The second partner responds with his or her perspective on the clause just read, before going on to the second or third.

EXERCISE 5:
A COMMUNICATIONS CHECKLIST_____

Instructions. We often take communication for granted and allow our communication skills to go untested. Frequently we score ourselves on our capacity to communicate clearly quite differently than our partner would rate us.

The following checklist is a useful exercise in rating your own skills and comparing the rating with your partner's estimate of your abilities.

1. Read through the check list and give yourself a rating on the scale of one to five—one being "poor," five being "outstanding."

2. Then rate your partner's communication skills using the same scale.

3. Now compare. Each of you take time to report how you see the other. Note the discrepancies between your self report and your partner's report on your communication behavior.

4. Be aware of your feelings during this exercise. Do you find it increases your openness to hear the other or invites any defensiveness?

5. Notice how you communicated during this exercise. Did you exhibit any of the communication styles you like or dislike? Discuss.

A COMMUNICATIONS CHECKLIST

1. I realize that what I see is an incomplete picture of what might be observed. I see in part; I know in part.   1 2 3 4 5

2. I recognize that my perspective is private, personal, partial, not wholly right or fully wrong.   1 2 3 4 5

3. I realize that what people say to me about a situation or a person is a condensed version of what might be said.   1 2 3 4 5

4. I realize that my expectations, interests and feelings will filter what I see, affect what I hear and bias what I say.   1 2 3 4 5

5. I focus my communication sharply, attempting to make intent and impact match as nearly as possible.   1 2 3 4 5

6. I am alert to nonverbal signs of misunderstanding and I adjust to such silent feedback by restating and improving.   1 2 3 4 5

7. I show that I am glad to have a listener ask questions or restate my message to check out my meaning.   1 2 3 4 5

8. I avoid ultimate language and "allness" by quantifying and qualifying whenever possible.   1 2 3 4 5

9. I use words expressing degress of difference when possible rather than two-value words.   1 2 3 4 5

10. I speak for myself, from myself in clear "I positions." I use "we messages" only to express what has been jointly agreed or is commonly accepted.   1 2 3 4 5

11. I try to understand what a speaker means in terms of his/her frame of reference, before I react to the statement.   1 2 3 4 5

12. I am aware of whether I am stating observations, feelings, interpretive inferences or value judgments.   1 2 3 4 5

13. I avoid using words that trigger "signal reactions" so that the other will be free to respond to what I say, not to how I said it.   1 2 3 4 5

14. I recognize I have only an inkling of what the other means, so I check out my hunch until the other agrees that I have "heard."   1 2 3 4 5

5
ROLES

ROLES:

COMPLE-MENTARY	SYMMETRICAL	PARALLEL	INTERTWINED
I YOU AM ARE I ME	I YOU AM vs ARE I YOU	YOU we I ARE are AM YOU we I	you WE i are ARE am you WE i
We are THE DREAM.	We are my dream; we are not yours.	We have a joint dream.	We share our dreams.
IDENTITIES DEPENDENT	IDENTITIES COUNTER-DEPENDENT	IDENTITIES SEPARATE	IDENTITIES SHARED
ROLE CLARITY	ROLE COMPETITION	ROLE DEFINITION	FUNCTION SHARING
We each have our own role and responsibilities.	We seek balanced roles and equal rights.	We are free to define roles.	We share functions with little thought of rules.

Jim and Jan met in college.

She was pretty, vivacious, outgoing, exciting.

He was shy, plain, absorbed in his studies and work, engrossed in his professional preparation and success.

They marry. She drops out of her work as an artist to have three children. He invests himself deep in his work. She suffers long periods of loneliness, feeling "trapped at home," struggling with anxiety, depression, inability to care for home or children. He has become totally committed to his work. Finally, after seven years of marriage, they see a counselor.

They enter, he sits in a stiff "computer" style. She slumps into a "placater" position, speaks first, gradually takes a "blamer" position. He acts kind and generous, conceals his resentment, remains factual, logical, reasonable.

She is anxious, depressed, resentful of home responsibility, irritable towards children, angry at his coldness, inability to love and emotional unavailability.

He intellectualizes automatically, shows no emotion, expresses few feelings, shows little capacity for intimacy, but points out the family (his) success and security.

As their conversation unfolds, her blaming evokes his defensiveness. His countercharges trigger her anger and the two are into a 'tis/'taint, yes you did/no I didn't cyclical conflict.

What is happening here?

These two people on a seesaw, Jim and Jan, couldn't have been more complementary. Like two sailors each leans on opposite sides to keep the boat from tipping.

But the complementary marriage is breaking up.

The two are becoming symmetrical. They are squaring off in opposite corners of the ring for a 10-round match. Their conflicts are tit for tat, blow for blow, plot and counterplot. Their second marriage is breaking upon them.

Marriage is like cycling.

In the first stage of marriage, the two are riding the same bike. Often one rides the handlebars while the other pedals. The dependent partner goes along while the dominant partner supplies the power.

In the second marriage, the pedaler drops the rider, or the rider kicks the pedaler off, but they both compete for the same bike, for the right to steer direction, for the control of speed and brakes.

In the third stage, separate bikes allow them to differentiate. Now they ride side-by-side, regulating their speed, choosing their common direction. They ride separately together. Each supplies her own power, each keeps his own bike going. Sometimes in tandem, one may ride ahead, or lag behind, but each keeps the other in sight or in mind.

In the fourth marriage, they may be ready for a bicycle-built-for-two. Then both can supply equal power, or one can rest without being left behind, but they ride individually, together.[1]

These four marriages are expressed in the sequence of roles which are complementary, competitive, cooperative and finally collaborative. These are best described as complementary, symmetrical, parallel and intertwined.

Complementary Marriage

"Born with a good mouth, I found someone who had great ears. I loved his ability to listen appreciatively, then I came to resent his silence. He enjoyed my expressiveness, until he became exhausted with my words."

"For me, getting my work done on schedule—my schedule—has to come before everything else. So her ability to be spontaneous and impulsive, to drop everything when excitement calls, was a wonderful antidote to my drivenness.

"But I hated it when she mothered me, though I probably asked for it. I had lost my mother when I was seven, so I grew up with my dad and three brothers. I married an oldest daughter who had helped raise six younger kids. I guess I knew what I needed."

In marriage, "two become one," and it is only a matter of time until it is clear which one. The early fusion allows the two to merge all the way into their solid-core-self. This temporary process allows the two to test out their own strengths and weaknesses, but should begin diminishing in the second or third year of life together.

The complementary matching of couples can be uncanny, the impulsive marries the disciplined, the inhibited is drawn to the expressive, the dominant to the submissive. The undeveloped side in oneself is modeled and supplied by the partner. In a growing relationship, the otherness excites and stimulates the completion of oneself; in a frozen dependency, the two exaggerate each other's tendencies and frustrate themselves.

"Complementarity" is spoken of in different ways:

First, as the "fit" that many couples experience between contrasting personality traits. Your dynamism enlivens me; my patience is a helpful balance to your enthusiasm. Or, your colorful contrasts in mood excite the monotony of my stable flatness of feelings.

Second, complementarity is frequently defined as the innate differences between *all* men and *all* women. The differences lie between complementary genders, not between unique individuals. In this view, each of us fits into one of two categories with "given" characteristics which fortunately complete one another. This view of complementarity denies rather than celebrates individual differences. If males are males, with little variation; and females are females, with few complications, then there's little to explore, little room for growth.

Third, complementarity may refer to the mysterious way in which persons from different family systems, with both similarities and differences find each other and marry. The mutual attraction is based on surface similarities—interests shared in common—and deep differences. These profound contrasts which draw them together provide a psychological complementarity which meets both personal and familial needs. For the persons, the selected mate offers a balance to deeper trends in the personality, a balance which promises to fulfill missing or undeveloped parts of the self. For the two families merging, the chosen person may fulfill a needed role or a missing element which completes an unrecognized gap in the family's makeup.

Complementary relationships fit together in the same manner that one hand washes another, that male and female bodies fit and complete each other. But these anatomical metaphors are of unchangeable characteristics, whereas most personality traits that complement one another not only could, but should be free to change. The early interlocking should function to model and invite growth for each other, not to make each a copy of the other, but rather to become complete in our own uniquely balanced ways.

When complementary relationships become fixed they are most often supported by the belief that in any dyad, one must define or lead and the other be defined or follow:

"I'm in charge now," the one may say nonverbally.

And the other replies, "That's OK with me."

Or one may rescue and save while the other enjoys the

COMPLEMENTARY MARRIAGE

Role Clarity

We each have our own roles,
we each know our place,
task, responsibilities.

Identities Dependent

We gain our identities
from each other and from
our other relationships,
so identity is dependent
although one may appear
independent.
Identity is defined by
role, such as parent, partner,
profession, performance.

Conflict Suppressed

The paired problems of
dominance/submission,
aggression/accommodation,
seduction/attraction,
blaming/placating,
computing/distracting
lead to one-way overt
settlement with two-way
covert exchange.

I am I—You are Me too.
We are *The Dream*

Figure 1

dependency and attention: "I need someone to rescue to feel good about myself."

"How fortunate, since I am looking for a savior."

These beliefs are usually several generations deep, and so are beneath conscious awareness. People can live "as if" they are invalids who need another to validate them even while they hate, fight or resent anyone noticing what is taking place.

Complementary relationships protect the contracts between the two people and go on maximizing the differences as if this polarization were fulfilling to themselves and the marriage. There are definite pay offs to this hand-and-glove contract. Coordination of activities is easier to attain and maintain since each soon knows his or her place. Once each has accepted an "up" or "down" position in a particular aspect of their relationship, then cooperation is more automatic and collaboration is simple since one is expected to lead, the other to follow.

In conflict, the participants choose matching styles. For example, one may exercise aggressive control and the other express accommodating niceness. The authoritarian demands of one partner are met with complying niceness. So *A* demands, and *B* submits; then *B* seduces, and *A* yields. Generally there will not be one powerful and one powerless mate. More often two kinds of power prevail: the overt power is visible as dominance, the covert power is less visible and usually far more powerful. Since it rules by the guilt evoked from martyrdom or misuse it may be extremely potent beneath the facade of impotence. You cannot *not* be powerful—the issue is how much, what kind of and which form of power is exercised in the relationship.

During the complementary period of marriage, a certain safety and security lies in conflict since partners can predict outcomes from the definite images they have of the other's responses under stress. The certainty that one will wield obvious power and the other yield to exercise covert power makes the end predictable and safe. But the negative impact can be sharp and deep. Both persons lose measures of freedom since one invariably submits and the other predictably dominates or directs. Change, development, and creative marital evolution throughout the life cycle is blocked.

When complementary roles become fixed, identities become dependent on these definitions of who we each are and what we are together. Even though the one may appear independent and the other dependent, both are defining identity from the partner and the partnership. Once a couple settles into a complementary marital style, the possibility of staying with it for life is always there.

Many relationships which look complementary on the surface may be collusions, not cooperative unions. Instead of freely exchanging their strengths and weaknesses, and dealing lovingly with temporary dependencies, the couple gets locked into fixed roles. This unconscious conspiracy for one partner to take responsibility for the other, and for the other to expect someone to care for him/her blocks both parties' growth.

Some of these collusions are commonly seen, as in the following:

"I'll be the parent—you be the child. I'll police support, nurture; you be spontaneous, carefree, childlike. I'll be the worker, you be the player."

"I'll be responsible—you can be irresponsible. The concern for managing our schedules, time, money, talent will be mine. You go ahead and follow your impulses freely. I'll be protector—you be protected."

"I'll be the healthy one—you be the sick one. I'll nurse

MARITAL TRADE-OFFS

Mate selection
is made with
exquisite
accuracy,
and unconscious
deals are made.
"I will be
your conscience
if you will
act out my impulses."[2]

To continue this list of marital
trade-offs.

"I'll be your parent
if you will be the child."
"I'll be responsible
if you will be impulsive."
"I'll be the helper
if you will act helpless."
"I'll be the servant
if you will be protector."
"I will be the leader
if you will be follower."
"I'll be the social animal and
you may play distant/withdrawn."

The variations on this theme are endless.

Figure 2

you, take care of your needs—you may act out the patient role. I'll be helper—you be helpless."

"I'll be the leader—you be the follower." Someone has to go ahead, the other follow; someone has to be in charge, the other adapt; someone has to have the last word, the other yield.

"I'll be the taker—you be the giver." In coercive marriages this may be "I'll be the tyrant—you be the victim." In more civil relationships, such expressions translate to "I'm here to serve—you are here to be served."

"I'll be the social one—you may be withdrawn. I'll take care of our communal, church, school obligations and you do your work, your art, your sports or whatever. I"ll be friendly—you be distant."

"We've never had any conflict," a veteran of 40 years in marriage said, "I don't understand why you talk about fighting, about conflict in marriage. We've never had any reason to fight."

"How did you carry it off, never having conflict?"

"Well, she always did what I asked her to do."

"How did that agree with you?" I asked his wife.

"Well, he always bought me whatever I wanted."

Complementary marriages were undergirded in the last generation by (a) a common-sense psychology which saw males and females as stereotypically matching and effective marriages as balanced unions of incomplete persons: (b) a practical sociology which saw male and female roles as given, unchanging, and as interlocking and completing as yin and yang; (c) a marital theology which saw man as "the head of the family," woman as "a helper who is to submit and support." So cultural and religious expectations reinforced couples staying in the first stage of marriage for life.

As we near the end of the twentieth century, the

expectations placed on marriage are much more expressive, emotional, relational than in previous periods. We expect levels of intimacy and openness, an expectancy which continually tends to shorten the length of time spent in the complementary period. The movement toward equality in roles and mutual sharing of parenting, housekeeping and home management moves couples from the automatic complementarity of early bonding into the symmetrical division of labor, negotiation differences and resolution of conflicts. This, for many, facilitates the earlier move toward parallel relationships.

However, most couples begin by living out the rules of their families of origin blended with those they are able to negotiate and create. These rules may be largely assumed and accepted, yet they are powerful determinants of the shape the marriage takes.

> Any rule established by a couple defines a certain type of relationship. A rule that a husband is to comfort his wife when she is in distress defines a relationship as complementary. Similarly an agreement that the wife is to have equal say about the budget is a mutual definition of a symmetrical relationship in that area.[3]

Every relationship is, in some respects, complementary; in others, symmetrical; and in still others, parallel. One of these patterns will be dominant in the first, second and third marriage within a marriage. We turn now to the second.

Symmetrical Marriage

"I would like equal time when we talk. I get tired when you go on and on."

"Maybe I do talk more than you, but one line from you is often worth a whole paragraph from me."

"I've felt taken for granted. It's time I got an equal chance to finish my education. I'm going back to school this fall."

"I don't feel like my point of view is respected in our decisions. I think this one should go the way I've been leaning."

"I'm willing enough to consider that, but I'm the one left out the last time."

When the perfect pair begins to discover that they are tired of interlocking roles, they become symmetrical.

Symmetrical relationships are like an emotional seesaw, a marital tug-of-war. They express the belief that both persons have equal right to define their relationship in all areas: "I have just as much right to define us as you do. My point of view is just as good as yours."

For the first stage of marriage, each partner has claimed his or her turf, and defined that part of the relationship unilaterally. Now the rights to each part of their life are contested as both are breaking out of the bondage of old roles. Each wants equality, so the differences we used to maximize to complement each other are now minimized. We are equally capable, equally entitled to direct our life together.

Some couples move through this symmetrical stage of marriage in great good humor, the jesting and joking turns the sparing and tussling into a time of amusing refurnishing of their marriage. But for others, the competition may be filled with tension and threat. Still others may be coolly mathematical in working out perfect fairness in the power-and-status struggle.

Symmetrical conflicts happen from the start of a marriage, but in the period from the seventh to the tenth year, the two discover a need to cut deeply into the basic expectations and assumptions of the marriage and readjust inequities. Often these injustices are continuations of both families of origin. He has a picture of his role that conflicts with hers; she has an image of her role that contrasts with his; both have expectations of their spouse's role that may fit the roles their parents played but not the present relationship.

When symmetrical conflict is positive and effective, the two partners can work for mutual, equal, balanced resolutions to their working, living and loving relationships. When it turns negative, two persons strive to claim the same turf, use the same strategies, compete for the same opportunities. At its more intense moments, much energy is put into rejecting the other's point of view and proving the superiority or the equal dignity of one's own.

Some couples get into symmetrical competition and conflict in early marriage and remain in this reciprocal dance all life long. This uproar marriage begins with superficial hassles over issues of preference, evolves into deeper conflicts over roles, then matures into relational conflicts, decade by decade. Two such weary battles can sustain marital conflict over the years as a way of hurdling the mutual dependency that is threatened by too much closeness—so fight for distance—and terrified of too much distance—so fight again to get enmeshed.

For almost a third of couples in Western culture, the first moves toward symmetrical conflict are seen as evidence of incompatibility, and so begins the slow or rapid movement toward separation and divorce.

When anger triggers anger, and confrontation by either gets a confrontive response, then conflict escalates.

In the symmetrical period both persons become anxious, both get caught up in the tensions, both feel the accelerating dissonance and distance results. Many couples can only tolerate tension in their relationship for a matter of weeks before they begin looking for the exit. When one considers that the symmetrical marriage within a marriage most often lasts for several years, not uncommonly from the seventh to the tenth, it is no surprise that emotional, physical and marital separations occur so frequently.

To work through this period takes courage. It also requires a determination to see a marriage through the worst of times as well as the best of times. And it demands a commitment to permanence and faithfulness in marriage. Those who survive move into the next stage—gradually for most, rapidly for a few—and find themselves moving in parallel paths or, as many describe it, walking parallel along the same path.

In early marriage, one chose the path; the other cooperated. In middle marriage the struggle over which road to take has almost divided them. Now they are ready to claim a common pathway wide enough for two and walk it side by side. No longer face-to-face in conflict, or back-to-back in defiance, they are free to be side by side.

Parallel Marriage

"I don't know how or when the change took place, but we weren't on opposite sides any more. We were back together again, but with a real difference from our early marriage. Now I felt so much more certain of who I was, so much more clear as to who you are, so much more confident about who we are together."

Parallel relationships, unlike the complementary puz-

SYMMETRICAL MARRIAGE

Role Competition

We seek balanced roles with equal rights to define task, privilege and responsibility.

Identities Counterdependent

We are dependent on each other for our identity, although we are constantly asserting and defending our independence in search of an equilibrium.
Identity is connected to or threatened by role, career, performance, success, recognition.

Conflict Cyclical

The balancing of two symmetrically paired persons with a fixed or rigid view of equality creates cyclical conflict with persons alternating in dominance/submission, initiating/responding and so on.

I am I.		You are You,
We are	vs.	not your
my dream.		dream.

Figure 3

zle pieces of the first marriage or the seesaw of the second, are like two walking hand in hand. Their separateness is symbolized by each walking on his or her own feet. Their direction is shared, side by side, their face a common goal. Their relatedness is certain and consistent as their hands touch and hold fast, each to the other.

Parallel relationships are based on the conviction that the recognition of differences, the appreciation of differentness and the expression of differing opinions can occur in give and take.

When it is clear that I have full right to be I, and you are fully entitled to be you, then we no longer need to worry that we will be swallowed up by our togetherness. Safe in our mutual respect we may explore our contrasting selves.

If I know that you not only tolerate but you can also appreciate my differentness, then I am more free to change and grow. We change, not when we are trying to reject, fight, or flee what we have been, but when we fully accept and own who, where, what we were and are. We free our partner to proceed in his or her self-chosen path of change by accepting her as she is, by giving up any fantasies or strategies of changing him from what he was and is.

No longer do they struggle for control. Each has separate areas of control to which the other defers; control is shared in joint issues. Their style of relating is more relaxed and confident. The patterned responses of the old symmetrical dance have come to an end. No longer rigid and reactive, they can be complementary in those areas where they augment each other; symmetrical where they need to work out new justice and fairness; and now parallel where shared relationship sets them both free to be autonomous selves in the solidarity of mature marriage.

When tensions rise, the conflict may rubber-band them back to a complementary solution. This is appropriate when the one person's strength is obvious in the face of the other's weakness. More often we commute between parallel and symmetrical styles. One day we are working things through with relaxed mutuality, the next we may slip back into a 'tis/'taint, yes/no, either/or competitive hassle. The crucial thing is, when we do regress to the old styles, that we recognize what is happening and spend less time in outdated patterns. Ten minutes of competitive conflict, where we used to spend 10 hours, or 10 days is a significant advance.

In its positive form, a parallel relationship allows each to develop a separate portion of their joint goals. There may be contrasting pathways and utterly different means used, but the two share the results in their common life.

In its negative mode, the relationship between the two may move in divergent lines, not parallel, and gradually grow apart. A vital marriage in this stage is connected by clear understandings, consistent covenants, shared time and mutual loyalty. These unite the two while respecting their separateness. Union is secure while separation is guaranteed.

The poet Rainer Maria Rilke described loving relationships as loving the other as well as loving the distance between the two which both connects and separates. This distance guarantees closeness and contact yet insures respect for the sanctity of the other. Love is the tension between union and separation, according to theologian Paul Tillich. Union symbolizes the drive to merge and melt into the loved one; separation recognizes the necessity for honoring the other's boundaries and inviolable dignity. Love is moving as close to another as is possible without violating the other's personhood; love is making authentic

PARALLEL MARRIAGE

Role Definition
We are free to define roles
according to preference and
ability without pressure or
threat.

Identities Separate
We are each persons with
individuated identities,
personal awareness of worth,
power, freedom of choice,
change and flexibility.
Identity is separating from
doing (my work) and having
(my stuff) and growing in being
(mySELF)

Conflict Negotiated
The parallel presence of two
centered persons allows them
to deal with the contrast of
differences and the clash of
similarities in equal negotiation.
As old cycles or binds recur,
they are worked through to
mutually satisfactory solutions.

YOU	we	I
ARE	are	AM
YOU	we	I

Figure 4

Once the realization
is accepted
that, even between
the closest human beings,
infinite distances
continue to exist,
a wonderful living
side by side
can grow up,
if they succeed
in loving the distance
between them
which makes it possible
for each to see the other
whole
and against
a wide sky![4]

contact with the other without attempting control or dependence, domination or seduction.

Side by side, each loving the other, both prizing the distance between them which unites and separates, the two move confidently down a shared path toward a common goal. As they travel, the need to remain equal is satisfied and then assumed, the concern to be perfectly matched in privilege and responsibility is fulfilled and largely forgotten. Now the two move more freely, in a pattern of their own unique dance. An intertwined relationship of freedom and intimacy is emerging.

Intertwined Marriage

"I feel really close to you, but in such a relaxed way. How different than early marriage when being close meant someone was being swallowed, or being apart felt like rejection."

In a mature marriage—if you should reach that stage—is a freedom to be near and far, distant and close, together and alone without anxiety going up and down. Each person has become clear in identity, so each feels safe in the closeness of intimacy. The interlocking interwoven patterns of their lives do not threaten either person's sense of selfhood. Identity work begins in adolescence, takes form in the 20s, is internalized in the 30s, tested in the crucible of marital conflict and growth during the 40s, and at last is secure in the 50s. It's a long time to wait for the full formation of identity, but the development of a solid-core self requires time and life experience.

In earlier stages, one's identity is connected to performance, then to career achievement and then to roles and station in life. But as identity is centered in per-

INTERTWINED MARRIAGE

Function Sharing
We share, exchange, delegate, assign and reassign functions without thought of roles.

Identities Shared
As persons with clear identities and centered selfhood, we are free to be near and far, together and separate, knowing we are secure and accepted.

Identity is centered in personhood, disconnected from role, career achievement, performance.

Conflict Utilized
Conflict is accepted, welcomed, utilized to invite growth and deepen relationship. It is no longer feared as destructive but celebrated as constructive excitement and energy for growth.

you	WE	i
are	ARE	am
you	WE	i

Figure 5

sonhood, it is disconnected from role, performance and position. As these are separated from the solid self, roles are laid aside, and people become free to see tasks not as roles but as functions. Now functions can be shared, exchanged, delegated, assigned and reassigned with little thought of roles.

The roles, which once were assigned by their traditions and expectations, then debated and disputed in middle marriage and at last accepted with concern for equal justice in the parallel period, now are largely dropped. When seen as functions rather than roles the same tasks look so much different.

The role perspective sees tasks and persons as inseparable; the function attitude recognizes that people choose certain tasks and refuse others, that no tasks belong to one sex and not the other, except gestation and breast-feeding. All others can be assigned, exchanged, shared, renegotiated according to gift, preference or other circumstance. Now the two experience an openness and a freedom that allows their lives to move near and far without threat of either abandonment or engulfment.

The parallel period, which prized the distance between them as an essential part of the justice, respect and balance of the relationship, has been superseded by the joyful intertwining of lives in the mature marriage of two secure selves.

Perhaps the best metaphor for the interwoven character—not enmeshed—of two intertwined lives is the dance.

Anne Morrow Lindbergh has written a delightful poetic description of a mature relationship in her book of reflections, *Gift from the Sea*. It is quoted in this chapter. She notes the freedom and spontaneity of the dance as well as the rules and patterns of the couple's movement. There is confident ease, intricate patterning, relaxed trust, gentle closeness, intimate union.

They share the music; they feel the rhythm; they know the steps; they delight in improvising; they excite and fulfill each other.

The last marriage is the best. It is worth living toward, working for, struggling after. I have become truly I, you have grown to be fully you, and now the WE has become a thing which is truly greater than the sum of its parts. The i and the you can truly be written in lowercase letters, the **WE** has become bold face and capital.

The first we-ness of fusion which was destroyed in the competition of separation and individuation was regained in the second we-ness of parallel security. Now the third we-ness has come (we 1, we 2 and we 3). As each has found the center and made it firm, the partners can meet freely and safely in a union which honors their distinctness as persons with less need for distance to defend their differentness.

EXERCISE 6: TAKING AN I-POSITION _____

Instructions. Taking a clear position as a "single I" is a process of ongoing development and growth. It is helped by each person speaking from the self, for the self without blaming or apologizing, without excusing or explaining, without attacking or defending. The clearest and most helpful way of increasing your capacity to speak from a firm "I-position" is to use "I-messages."

I-messages are not egotistical messages of self-imposing arrogance. They are self-disclosing, vulnerable, confessional statements of what I think, feel, see, want, choose and plan to do in response to you.

A good relationship
has a pattern
like a dance
and is built
on some
of the same
rules.

The partners
do not need
to hold on tightly,
because they move
confidently
in the same pattern,
intricate
but gay
and swift
and free,
like a country dance
of Mozart's . . . .

There is no place here
for the possessive clutch
the clinging arm,
the heavy hand;
only the barest touch in passing.

Now arm in arm,
now face to face,
now back to back—
it does not matter which.
Because they know they are partners
moving to the same rhythm,
creating a pattern together,
and being invisibly nourished by it.[5]

When my I-ness is secure
I can respect your you-ness.
When your you-ness is a given
You can enjoy my I-ness.
If my I-ness swallows your you-ness
or your you-ness diminishes my I-ness
then our we-ness is impoverished.
So I shall be I, you will be you,
and we are free to be we
in a dance of integrity and intimacy.

It is important for couples to practice the use of clear I-messages and to assist each other in expressing what is felt, wanted, needed with honesty and impact.

But note. Most people beginning to speak in I-messages only use them to conceal a hidden you-message, like "I feel angry because you don't . . . . " A clear I-message is not an analysis of the other, it speaks *only* of the self and for the self. Experiment in cleaning up your I-position until you can express what you feel and want without blaming, analyzing or describing the other's position or behavior.

Some people have trouble starting sentences with an "I" pronoun. The following stems have been found helpful to start making "I" statements. Please complete these sentences and start thinking about other possible completions of these sentences.

I wish _____

I would _____

I hate _____

I want _____

I feel _____

If I were _____

If I could _____

I love _____

I can _____

I could _____

I should _____

I ought _____

I enjoy _____

I must _____

I need _____

I like _____
I am pleased when _____
I understand _____
I see _____
I remember _____
I fear _____
I would be pleased if _____
I am _____
I trust _____
I hurt _____
I think _____
I do not like _____
I complain _____
I get scared when _____
I blame _____
I try _____
I work _____
I look _____
I do not want _____

Make up three stems on your own and complete them.

1. _____

2. _____

3. _____

EXERCISE 7: POSITIONAL EXERCISES _____

Instructions. Seven key parts of relationship emerge when

couples experiment with taking different physical positions and relational positions. The following exercise selects seven elements of daily communication and suggests that you intentionally experience them in depth.

Each part of the exercise invites you to explore a different aspect of how you relate now in the stage of marriage you are enjoying or not enjoying.

Enter this exercise with an attitude of "trying on" a different aspect of relationship to see how it is fitting or not fitting you at this period of your relationship.

These are offered as experiments, as ways to explore and deepen parts of yourselves and your communication.

No outcomes are prescribed. Both partners should feel and claim the right to act and speak in ways that are consistent with their personalities and congruent with their deeper selves. The hope is that each will discover something freeing, pleasurable and more effective in seeing, hearing, touching, naming and being with each other.

Communication Exercises

To deepen communication, experience your ways of giving and receiving messages slowly, bit-by-bit; reflectively, step-by-step; relationally, eye-to-eye.

Allow sufficient time to experience each element fully before proceeding to the next. After three minutes of silent experiencing, you may verbalize discoveries or responses.

1. Knee-to-knee

Sit knee-to-knee, close your eyes, meditate on the

relationship which connects the two of you. Who are you? Who is the other? What is this something that connects you? After three minutes, share your reflections.

2. Eye-to-eye

Silently allow the other to look deeply into your eyes. Drop any defensiveness you feel and allow them to enter. Be aware of your feelings as you receive the other's gaze and also of your interpretations of the other's feelings. Share discoveries.

3. Hand-to-hand

Join hands and communicate what you are feeling by your handclasp, by tracing the fingers, palm and wrists, by pressure or massage. Reflect on who initiates, who leads, who is more tender, more firm, more passive. Share.

4. Name-to-name

Take turns saying the other person's name in a wide variety of ways, changing tone, intensity, emotion and so on. Finally, each one alternate saying the other's name with respect and affection until the other signals that "it feels good." Report.

5. Feeling-to-feeling

One person shares something that she/he feels deeply about here and now. The other limits response to simply reporting perceptions of what the one is feeling. "You feel lonely when I'm more involved in my work than in the family and . . . . " Exchange roles. Repeat.

6. Back-to-back

Try arguing at a distance with your backs to each other. Choose an issue first, then turn and walk five paces. Stand for the duration of the duel. Be aware of the distance, the absence of facial and bodily cues, the feelings within, the process between you.

7. Face-to-face

Now repeat the argument issue while standing face-to-face at the distance preferred by each. Meet nose-to-nose, then each back up to the distance that feels comfortable for both. Be aware of changes in feelings in these two positions. Compare the absence and presence of eye contact and all the facial/physical signals. Report your discoveries.

Now sit knee-to-knee, hand-in-hand and reflect eye-to-eye on your discoveries from these seven experiences of hearing and being heard.

6

INTIMACY

INTIMACY:

BONDING

The two merge in intense affectional intimacy. A primary sense of we-ness is welded.
(We)

BALANCING

The two separate in cyclical conflictual intimacy. A fully mature sense of identity is being achieved.
(I-You)

BLENDING

The two integrate their lives in a mutually intimacy. Identity is separate, solidarity is secure.
(I-We-You)

BECOMING

The two mature in multilevel intimacy. Free to be themselves they are becoming.
(We)

DEPENDENT

Intimacy is co-dependent. Closeness is dependent on the moment; the situation on each other's "acting as prescribed."

INDEPENDENT

Intimacy is intermittent. It is intense when all is going well, absent when tension or threat is present.

INTER-DEPENDENT

Intimacy is integrative as autonomy is clear, solidarity secure, mutuality experienced.

INTIMATES

Intimacy is authentic. Closeness and understanding develops in emotional, mental, social and spiritual levels.

Ann

"Do you know the Aesop's Fable of the ant and the grasshopper? The ant works and stores for the winter, the grasshopper feasts and sings all summer? That's us. Ned is an ant—the king of the ants; he wants to save every cent possible so we will be secure in the threatening future.

"But I'm a grasshopper. I want to enjoy life, to live now, not tomorrow. Maybe Ned can postpone living indefinitely, but I can't. For him, life is all working and sacrificing and saving.

"My parents were so afraid of not having enough money when they got old—they grew up in the depression—that they denied themselves anything that looked like pleasure.

"I'd like to be close to Ned, like we were during the first years of marriage when we were in graduate school, but now he's not available. He's working. All the time."

Ned

"I love Ann, she's the excitement, the real center of my life. I want her to have everything that her family had, and mine didn't. So I couldn't turn down a job that guarantees our security.

"Sure I work a lot of overtime. Yes, I have to be away traveling a good deal, but we have to sacrifice now if we want security tomorrow.

"Ann is not happy if I'm not there for all the things she plans. I can't stand to argue with her, so I try to be available when I can, I'm probably relieved when I'm scheduled to be away.

"The hassle over our time together—or the absence of it—and over my work just wears me out. It's like a wall between us. Until I get a promotion, I don't see how any of this is going to change."

We have a deep longing for intimacy. We have a deep fear of intimacy. So all the intimacy moves in two directions. Not a simple movement toward togetherness, it paradoxically enriches both separateness and connectedness.

I (being truly myself) can only be intimate with you as you are you (being truly yourself). Our intimacy increases as you are able to become more fully who you are, and I become more freely who I am.

In marriage, the two have been said—for centuries—to become one. In a matter of months it becomes obvious which one.

"In a traditional confluent marriage," Laura Perls observed, "the spouse is not a significant other but an insignificant same."

More than just a caricature, this description is a portrait of much marriage in which selfhood is lost in the merger. "Two people can either 'marry' or they can 'join.' When people 'join,' the separateness between them is ever present. The impossible relationship is to 'marry': to be totally known and know the other, to merge and be as close as possible. To 'marry' is like creating a sauce—its various ingredients are so well blended that they are indistinguishable. The opposing image is of two pieces of a jigsaw puzzle that join, but the seam is a separateness that cannot be overcome."[1]

True intimacy is found by linking not forging. Healthy relationships are not in contact, not continuous. Intimacy, paradoxical as it seems, is increased by our recognition of separateness, not by our denial of it.

The Paradoxes of Intimacy

Yes, intimacy has its paradoxical aspects:

One, a person needs to be separate in order to be close.

Two, the ones we love have the greatest power to hurt us.

Three, we must seek comfort and healing from those we hurt and who hurt us.[2]

These three paradoxical dimensions are central to intimate marriage. They are the puzzles of closeness, crisis and reconciliation.

Only separate selves are intimate together.

In order to be close to one's partner, one must become a separate self. Separation and togetherness are most often expressed as an either/or situation, but that is false; they are best understood as a both/and situation.

We are *both* becoming more separate selves with a clear sense of identity *and* we are *both* able to come together without fear or reservation.

We are *both* distinct as centered persons *and* we are *both* fulfilled in our blending together in shared emotional experience.

So *both* distinctness *and* connectedness, *both* union *and* separation, *both* twoness *and* oneness, *both* self-identity *and* marital unity are central to intimacy.

The dean of family therapists, Carl Whitaker writes of this in his typically pungent style.

> "As two people live together . . . then they grow closer together and farther apart at the same rate. This is a weird kind of business, but the closer they get, the more separate they are. If they don't grow more separate, they can't grow closer. If they can't increase their individuality, they can't increase their oneness . . . the more you are free to be with others,

> your wife specifically, significant others, the
> more you are free to be with yourself. The
> more you are with you the more you can be
> with her.[3]

Our first experiences of togetherness as a child are in symbiosis. We are continuous with the significant others, in primary fusion we must outgrow as we become separate selves. Fritz Kunkel called this the journey from We-1 through the discovery of I-Thou to the achievement of We-2.[4] Maturing is directly related to our emerging from being enmeshed into others, from losing our selfhood in others, from getting hooked by others, from feeling fused to others and becoming free to be with others as distinct and differing persons.

The central development that sets us free is the capacity to *be* with others without our needing to *do* something to earn, win or fulfill real or imagined expectations, or without their needing to *do* something to make us feel accepted or worthful.

To truly *be* with someone in intimacy, there are no requirements governing appearance, compliance or performance. Availability, presence and integrity of covenanting are all that is required. The commitment to *be* there for the other and with the other is what brings us together while recognizing our covenanting selves as separate responsible agents.

This commitment is not without fears. To let go and simply *be* together can evoke a whole family of fears, among which are the five major fears blocking intimacy.

> a. *the fear of merger.* If we move closer, I will
> feel engulfed, absorbed, swallowed up, so I
> must be on guard.

b. *the fear of exposure.* If we move closer, I will feel undressed and embarrassed, exposed and shamed, so I must be closed when close.

c. *the fear of attack.* If we move closer, I may be attacked, injured, penetrated, violated. So I must be cautious.

d. *the fear of abandonment.* If we move closer, I may open myself only to be left hanging, risk myself only to be ignored or rejected.

e. *the fear of one's own destructive impulses.* If we move closer, I may not be able to control the anger I feel, or the disgust at parts of you that I try not to think about, but I fear is there about to break out.

As I become more and more at peace with myself, my fears of being absorbed, exposed, attacked, abandoned, or explosive go down. My confidence that I can safely and freely be my whole self in your presence rises and grows. I can risk being spontaneous—not knowing what will come out but trusting it all the same.

We Only Hurt the Ones We Love

Intimacy makes us vulnerable to both hurt and love, to both invasion and rejection, to both invitation and affection. Lucianno and Beth L'Abate describe this paradox so well:

Hurt and caring are intrinsically interwoven. We oftentimes give those we love a license to hurt. Functionally speaking, we are rarely if seldom hurt by strangers. Hurt and fears of being hurt only result from the intensity of close relationships and not from superficial or transitory relationships. Hence, there are feelings that relate to our vulnerability in a caring relationship. We can all be let down, betrayed, deceived, rejected and abandoned.[5]

Intimacy is the courage to be vulnerable, the necessary strength to be weak together. There is no way to avoid hurt in a relationship, although we should try to minimize the possibility and grow in our ability to reduce its intensity, spread, and duration by work through the injury as soon as possible. Being vulnerable, as one fallible human with another, means that hurts are inevitable but not irreparable. We will be hurt by each other if we live with each other. Since both pleasure and pain are essential to being alive, we must learn to handle our hurts to enrich our joys. In fact, in working through our hurtness, we deepen our love.

Love is the creative tension between contact and withdrawal that keeps us coming back for more, yet drawing back to see the other clearly and respectfully. Love is the balance of union and separation that allows us to merge profoundly—and at times painfully—and to emerge as stronger more distinct persons. This is a hurtful as well as joyful process. When two people move into each other's inner world, there will be misunderstandings, mistakes, misfortunes that hurt.

We always hurt the ones we love, yet we also can be healed and helped by those we love and who love us. Perhaps we can be healed *only* by one whom we have hurt.

We Are Healed by Those We Hurt
Marriage is that strange and puzzling relationship in which, paradoxically, we need to seek comfort from the very per-

son who has been party to our hurting. If we cannot share our hurt feelings and allow the one who has hurt us to comfort us, we are endangering the whole relationship. When we have hurt each other, we must also be the agents of healing. Going outside the relationship for healing is a temporary process at best, a time of retreat for therapy that should return the comforting conciliating process to the two persons as quickly as possible.

The feelings of fear, pain, hurt, anger and the anxiety about further hurt all need to be shared if the relationship is to grow. The natural temptation is to ventilate these feelings in complaints about the past or in predictions and expectations about the future. This practice only intensifies the hurt and drives the two persons farther apart, positionally, while enmeshing them emotionally.

Both of these movements are in the wrong direction. Reconciliation occurs when we separate emotionally and move together positionally. When it is clear that I will stand with you, no matter what, and that I will recognize and honor your right to your feelings, then we are remaining in contact while respecting each other's uniqueness.

And that understanding is the secret of the healing relationship. When I am hurt, I am helped by those who stand with me—in genuine, accepting presence—but do not seek to fix my problem, clarify my confusion or heal my pain. Real healing comes from within, and those we love can call out that healer by being an invitation to reconciliation.

Intimacy is the sharing of hurt feelings, the acceptance of the one who is hurting and the working through of the hurt that lies between us. Deeper intimacy cannot be achieved only by sharing the positive and bonding experiences. If there is no resolution of negative and alienating elements in a relationship, there is no growth. All admiration and adulation does not create intimacy, it nourishes fantasy.

All resentment and irritation has little to offer either. But the resolution of our resentments, the integration of our irritations into our life together connects us at the levels of both our acceptable and unacceptable selves. When my full self can be known and validated, I am able to experience closeness with less and less facade. When your lovable and unlovable sides are permitted to express themselves without rejection, then you need not pretend what is not actual or pose as what is not authentic, spontaneous and natural.

The Two Sides of Intimacy

Intimacy is composed, not only of the three paradoxical elements we have just explored, but of many more.

Intimacy has a history; it is a sustained, lasting commitment with a stable duration over time. Intimacy is also a peak experience, a moment of close, joyous ecstasy.

Intimacy has stability; it is a constant trustworthy fidelity. Intimacy is also negotiable, adjustable, open to change and growth.

Intimacy is self-giving; it is serving and even sacrificing for the good of the other. Intimacy is also being oneself; it is discovering oneself in relationship.

Intimacy is caring; it is accepting and affirming the other. Intimacy is also differing, confronting and conflicting. It is caring and confrontation, anger and love.

Intimacy is openness; it is transparency and self-disclosure. Intimacy is also privacy; it honors secrets, respects solitude.

Intimacy is growth; it is exploring, unfolding and becoming. Intimacy is also relaxation, it is ease and comfortableness.

INTIMACY

Solidarity Issues
(closeness)

Autonomy Issues
(separateness)

Intimacy grown from shared history. There is no instant intimacy. It takes time to mature, deepen.

Intimacy requires intentional moments of deep sharing, of intense celebration, of joint ecstasy.

Intimacy is based on stability, on certainty of presence, on constancy.

Intimacy is enriched by an openness to renegotiation, a willingness to accept change.

Intimacy is nourished as another's needs are as important to me as my own.

Intimacy is supported by each person's claiming responsibility for meeting his/her own needs.

Intimacy is felt in the warmth of caring, in the genuineness of presence, in the accuracy of empathy.

Intimacy is deepened by risking or sharing differences, by confrontation with issues, by resolution of conflict.

Intimacy is enhanced by free self-disclosure and open transparency.

Intimacy is guaranteed by respecting each other's uniqueness, secrets, privacy.

Intimacy is increased by a commitment to explore, examine, grow in knowing and understanding the other person.

Intimacy is celebrated with greatest richness when there is relaxation, comfort, ease, harmony, an ability to "let it be."

Figure 1

Intimacy requires time; it does not grow if not given time to develop. Intimacy requires intense bonding; there must be moments of ecstatic welding, sharing, celebrating.

Intimacy requires clear understandings. If the covenant or contract is unclear, one-sided, fragile or easily terminated the closeness is limited. If it cannot be renegotiated in new circumstances, the trust is blocked.

Intimacy requires empathy that embraces each other's thoughts, feelings and actions. It equally requires that one feel her own feelings fully, think his own thoughts clearly and choose self-owned actions freely or the intimacy is superficial.

Intimacy requires self-disclosure by both parties, yet it also respects the autonomy and self-direction of each. It offers and welcomes transparency, yet it also respects and celebrates solitude and privacy.

Intimacy recognizes the reality of death, of human finitude, of frailty and of fallibility. It accepts the other as truly human, yet it is hopeful that love never ends and that our faithfulness to each other transcends suffering, death.

These paradoxical elements are expressed in figure 1 where the contrast between permanence and peak experience, stability and negotiability, service and self-discovery, caring and confrontation, openness and privacy, growth and relaxation are set out in table form. Both sides are necessary for authentic intimacy. Both are halves of the whole reality we've got to get together if we're going to get it together with each other.

If intimacy were a relationship we could achieve once for all, perhaps an art to be mastered and maintained for life, then we might take the preceding polarities as a map of the territory. But intimacy is not one state to be achieved, it differs in each stage of marriage. And in the four basic marriages within a marriage, intimacy moves from a first pattern to a more satisfying and complete second and third and fourth. We shall call these dependent, independent, interdependent, and fully intimate relationships of intimacy.

Bonding Intimacy

Marriage one: intimacy is co-dependent.
"Sometimes I feel so close to you. I can't explain why it happens when it does, but something brings us together. These moments of intense intimacy are a kind of serendipity. Maybe something you say or do brings back the memory of a special moment, and then I feel like the two of us are one."

Intimacy in early marriage is the bonding of two co-dependent persons both believing themselves to be independent. But their moments of intense togetherness are events they cannot share intentionally; happiness happens. Intimate moments cannot be chosen and offered to each other at any time; they break upon them when the time is right, the circumstances are perfect, the mood is congenial.

This view of intimacy as the romantic moment allows for fortuitous and unpredictable moments of closeness, but because it is dependent on all going well and everything coming together, there is no certainty of intimacy tomorrow.

Co-dependent intimacy may have great intensity in its moments of union, but it carries within itself the constant threat of distance and coldness. So both parties walk on eggs, denying the signs of tension and hoping for the mutual vibrations that will signal their togetherness.

ALWAYS CHANGING

i know that i am saying the opposite
of what i said last week
but please don't hold me to last week
or last month
because i am always changing
seeing things in a new light
rethinking
revising
reevaluating

if i can't go on changing like that
i will die to our love
if i have to adhere
to what i no longer believe
if i have to close my eyes
to new challenges and new obstacles
i will be consistent but stagnant and dead

i am unpredictable
i cannot promise you anything
i don't know what i will say next week
but
i have made the decision to love you
to share my life with you
and to do that i need the freedom to change
to remain alive in a creative love for you
my love
my friend[6]

In such bonding, intimacy is this mysterious affair of unexplainable and unpredictable emotional warmth that sweeps the two along. Wonderful as this sense of mystical romantic union may be, it needs more than the rush of emotion to last. Authentic intimacy is rooted in a depth of commitment that is tested and matured through the second marriage and into the third.

In this dependent period, we feel intimate when our expectations are fulfilled. We feel close when our dreams are being confirmed. We feel most close when The Dream appears to be coming true for us. But all these are intimacies based on having, not being; on achieving externals, not celebrating internal worth.

The co-dependence is self-destructive. Eventually one or both must make a move toward regaining the identity sacrificed in this too-easy solution of being enmeshed in each other. And with that first move, the two are springboarded into another marriage. The old intimacy begins to break up. It still returns—intermittently—only to be interrupted again and again.

Balancing Intimacy

Marriage two: intimacy is intermittent.

"Sure, we have some really good moments, but the struggle to work out equality is so difficult that the times when we understand each other and really get together are touch and go."

Intimacy is precarious during this second marriage. Both are struggling for equality, each is pressing for his or her own place in the sun, neither is free to move close for the intimacy they need. The two may be acting independent, but in many ways they are reacting as dependent persons. They see themselves as independent but actually they are counterdependent, that is, each counters every move toward the old easy intimacy of early marriage by pressing toward a separate sense of self.

Now conflict intimacy begins to develop. Although common sense sees these two words as contradictory, conflict can connect people deeply. The struggle to define an independent self pushes each toward sharper positions of autonomy. Yet they discover that every increase in autonomy makes possible a deeper sense of solidarity. When he feels more respect for her ability to take a clear position, he finds surprisingly a new depth to their meeting. When she sees his new firmness in self-definition, she feels a greater security in their moments of closeness. There is a clarity of understanding between people who have tested each other's mettle and found themselves and their opponent trustworthy. When we have fought with each other we may truly come to know each other.

During this marriage, the commuting between poles of separation and togetherness becomes more rapid—at times like a weaver's shuttle. As Sonia Nevis describes it, it is an impossible situation.

> The minute I get the separateness I want, I'm furious about it. The minute I get the combining I want, I'm stifled by it. So I keep swinging between the two. I can settle somewhere in the middle, but "settling" doesn't feel so good either. This is not the same in friendship. The distance that exists in friendship gives me everything I need. The situation in marriage is not the same . . . "I love you," we say, and we hug tight. We want to stay *attached* to the other

person, but we can't tolerate that. Marriage
opens us up to loving too much, and we have to
love *moderately*. If we love to our full capacity,
we set up an impossible situation."[7]

Loving too much leads to absorption, possessiveness,
jealousy, servitude and a host of other abuses of self and
other. Loving too little leads people down diverging paths
toward apathy, coexistence or estrangement.

Love and intimacy must discover a joining of fully separate selves, a blending of separate and distinct worlds. As
this emerges from the ruins of the old merger a third kind
of marital intimacy begins.

Blending Intimacy

Marriage three: intimacy is integrative.

"It's hard to explain, but I used to feel overwhelmed
when we were really close. There was too much togetherness. We could be close for a while, but then I needed to
come up for air. Now its like we've broken through to a
new level of togetherness that doesn't threaten our separateness."

When the struggle to be separate is nearly over, and
the drive to be an autonomous self with a clear sense of "I-
ness" has reached a point of clarity, the two find a new
freedom to move close again, to begin blending needs and
wants.

Maturity is measured by the freedom to both act inde-
pendently and to relate dependently. Although we rarely
express it that tersely, the ability to be both dependent
and independent at appropriate times and in fitting ways is
a mark of the fully functioning person. This balance of

INTIMACY: POLARITY OR PARADOX?

Rely on our history together.	1 2 3 4 5	Look for peak experience and spontaneity.
Rely on the stability and unchanging commitment.	1 2 3 4 5	Experiment with change, renegotiate commitments.
Feel close through meeting the other's needs in self-giving.	1 2 3 4 5	Feel free to meet one's own needs in self-care.
Feel intimate in times of support, acceptance and caring.	1 2 3 4 5	Feel real contact in times of differing, conflicting, confronting.
Feel close when self-disclosing, being open and transparent.	1 2 3 4 5	Feel free to prize ones own privacy, uniqueness, secrets.
Feel an ongoing need to grow, explore, keep moving together, to "work at it."	1 2 3 4 5	Feel a relaxation, a sense of ease and harmony, an ability to "let it be."

EARLY MARRIAGE (co-dependent intimacy) will often rate from 1 to 3 on most of these polarities.

MIDDLE MARRIAGE (independent intimacy) will rate from 3 to 5 as each searches for self-identity.

LATER MARRIAGE (interdependent intimacy) will rate down the middle as both seek to balance the polarities equally in parallel relationships.

MATURE MARRIAGE (intimacy) refuses to rate these as polarities, since they now recognize them as truly paradoxical, that both are equally necessary. You cannot have one without the other.

Figure 2

mutual give and take between two is what we call "interdependence." Each is able to act autonomously, both prefer mutuality; each can choose responsibly, both prefer to choose responsibly; each is fully functional alone, both prefer to share life together.

During the preceding stage, intimacy was sharply limited by the need to safeguard one's own identity. During this finalizing of identity, defensiveness is inevitable. The diagram of figure 2 shows the pendulum swing between an intimacy of solidarity in early marriage, an intimacy of autonomy in middle marriage and then the intimacy which emerges as interdependence. Separateness and connectedness are now brought into balance—the balance of mutual intimacy.

Intimates

Marriage four: the two are becoming authentic intimates.

"One night as we were out walking, we looked at each other, and asked how long we had been together. It had been 25 years. We had known that all along, but now we knew it in a deep sense of having *lived those years* deeply together. We laughed as we said, 'I guess we're survivors. The trial period is over, we fit together now!'"

Becoming authentic intimates is the marital part of what is characteristic of all mature personhood. Being is more important than doing or having, becoming is more exciting and nourishing than setting into consistent patterns of who I always was-am-will be as a person or a partner. One learns to live with fewer and fewer defenses. Why defend what I'm willing to revise and renegotiate? One risks living a more open-ended life together.

"I felt a sense of calm, of being at peace with each

other as well as with myself. It's a peace that has always been a part of our love, but now it is woven throughout our intimacy in an unexplainable way. When we are fully together on things it just feels right. And when we differ or disagree, it is all right too. I know we are both free to flow with life, to change and grow, so it's OK."

Becoming intimates requires time and shared history, and it also surprises a couple with experiences of intensity and vividness. What was previously experienced as two poles, drawing us in opposite directions, two poles that must be reconciled, integrated and balanced is now discovered to be a paradox. And paradox does not seek resolution but a circular experience of both sides, a continuing movement between both separation and union that does not compromise either you or your partner.

When the ironies of intimacy are experienced as paradox, then we can take a deep both/and attitude toward conflicts, tensions, competitions and contradictions. We *both* need *and* we don't need each other. Hopefully we can report our needs and negotiate appropriate satisfaction. We *both* love *and* hate each other. Finally we will discover that the parts we hate are necessary to discover that the parts we hate are necessary to personhood too, and we can accept them since the parts we love are so much greater. We *both* admire *and* resent each other's strengths—those things we admire in others are often the parts of ourselves we long to have and yet cannot claim, so we resent another's expression of them even as we admire them.

The listing of ironies that are present in every intimate relationship is a fascinating study of both personalities. As long as either or both persons fight them as foes or swing between them as polarities, they entrap us and limit the possibilities of mature intimacy.

Intimacy is the experience
of close sustained familiarity
with another's inner life.
In an intimate relation,
one beholds another person
in her essential depth,
in his innermost reality.
Intimacy is knowing another
from the inside out,
it is entering another's vision
and seeing through her eyes,
it is joining another's world
and walking through it on his feet.

Intimacy is only by mutual consent.
It is not possible in unilateral desire.
If one seeks closeness
with another who will have none of it,
then the relation is not intimate.
One may have intimate knowledge of another,
but not be intimate with the other.
Intimacy is the twofold flow
of caring and being cared about,
of loving and being loved,
of knowing and being known.[8]

Accepting them as delightful ironies, as perpetual paradoxical patterns in our relationship, lets us smile at what we thought were serious realities. Seeing the situation as less than tragic, perhaps comedic, allows us to enjoy the irony and employ the paradox as a resource for our ongoing growth.

Maturity is the ability to tolerate and then appreciate ambiguity. Maturity is the wisdom to see each other's maturation as complex, not simple, and well intentioned, not deliberately hurtful. Maturity is the recognition that life and love and I and you are paradoxical puzzles worth savoring, not solving.

Varieties of Intimacy

Many different kinds of intimacy are in a growing relationship. At the end of this chapter there will be an exercise for assessing, discussing and exploring your needs for greater intimacy in any or all of a rich variety or areas. But first it is useful for us to explore the most basic forms intimacy takes in marriage.

Five basic types of intimacy are often identified as (a) emotional, (b) intellectual, (c) aesthetic, (d) physical and (e) spiritual. There are more, as we will see later.

First, *emotional intimacy*. Two people are emotionally intimate when they both share similar feelings at the same time. The more completely mutual meeting of feelings, the greater the emotional intimacy. The most important conditions for emotional intimacy are: (1) that we do not need to apologize for, justify or defend our feelings; (2) that we appreciate each other's feeling world and support his right to feel as he does, her right to experience her own emotions.

Second, *intellectual intimacy*. When two people are intellectually intimate they meet eye-to-eye and mind-to-mind—with co-perceptions and co-interpretations. Two persons feel intimately understood when each can see what the other sees and can interpret the data in shared ways; then each feels deeply understood, and each is fulfilled by being understanding.

Third, *aesthetic intimacy*. Beauty can bring people together at a deep level of resonance and empathic oneness. The mutual appreciation of the aesthetically beautiful music, art, poetry, nature, liturgy, wonder and awe are all connective experiences, intimate experiences.

Fourth, *physical intimacy*. "Intimacy" is the commonly used euphemism for sexual contact. Much sexuality has the quality of intimacy, but genital activity can and often does take place without intimacy. At times, such activity is a violation of intimacy. Authentic sexual intimacy occurs when two people express a closeness, openness and genuineness with their bodies that reflects what is true of their lives. When we flow together in sexual delight that expresses and symbolizes the way we merge in emotions, thoughts, values and appreciation of beauty, then orgasm celebrates the union of lives and selves.

Fifth, *spiritual intimacy*. We can grow together on the most profound level by sharing our spiritual journey. Our worlds of faith, values, life meaning, life goals, motivation to love and serve can be both shared and separate. "Religion," as Alfred North Whitehead observes, "is what the individual does with his own solitariness."[9] In maturity, we welcome the solitude before God without fleeing the aloneness, and we share our solitudes without fear of being controlled or rejected. We can be truly *with* each other *before* God.

As one reflects on these five aspects of the intimate

relationship, the unmistakable leaps out—in our culture, sexual intimacy is seen as the fundamental, the central, the most crucial of all the intimacies. Because it is the visible, tactile, hormonal symbol that is also an emotional, spiritual aesthetic blending of two persons, it inevitably eclipses all the others. None of the others possesses the tangible, colorful, delightful, passionate immediacy and intensity of loving embrace which melts two persons into a state of emotional liquidity, yet each of them is an equal contributor to the total intimacy of marriage.

Novelist D. H. Lawrence writes of sex as an inclusive intimacy which must symbolize the whole of the relationship between a man and a woman and express the heart of the communication between them, yet not dominate the deeper movements of their souls. Sex is the volcanic eruptions of fire and light that represents the continental shifts along the emotional, spiritual, moral, aesthetic fault lines of the soul. His description of a long view of sex in marriage is worth reading and rereading together.

> For sex, to me, means the whole of the relationship between man and woman . . . that lasts a lifetime, and of which sex-desire is only one vivid, most vivid manifestation. Sex is a changing thing now alive, now quiescent, now fiery, now apparently quite gone . . . . A man says: I don't love my wife any more; I no longer want to sleep with her! But why should he always want to sleep with her? How does he know what other subtle and vital interchange is going on between him and her making them both whole, in this period when he doesn't want to sleep with her? And she, instead of jibing and saying that all is over and she must find another

man and get a divorce—why doesn't she pause,
and listen for a new rhythm in her soul, and look
for the new movement in the man?[10]

Perhaps the most succinct paradigm of intimacy is
found in the words of family therapist Virginia Satir. It
describes the wonderful mutual respect that flourishes
along the boundary between union and separation.

It can be read as polarities which must be kept in balance, if that is where you are in relationship. Or it can be
understood even more deeply as seven paradoxical conditions for loving intimacy.

Loving is holding another tenderly, yet not with clutch-
ing possessiveness. Still we are secure in the mutual own-
ership of our relationship, yet neither owns the other. Feel
the paradox?

Appreciation is both admiration and inevitably evaluation. We admire the good, the true, the beautiful in
another, yet without judging. Paradoxical.

Invitation is the most powerful form of communication,
yet it dares be a demand which seeks to manipulate or
control.

Being distant from each other allows us to reflect and
evaluate what is happening in our relationship from the
objectivity of distance, yet this can be in hopeful yearning
for growth not, say, punitive feelings of guilt.

Criticism and help can both be given and received as
gifts, not condemnation or insult.

All are paradoxical. Both sides are present in every
relationship, yet each corrects, clarifies and frees the
other to enrich love and intimacy.

Read and reread the poem to each other. Explore its
wisdom for renewing intimacy.

I WANT TO ...

Love you
    without clutching,
Appreciate you
    without judging,
Join you
    without demanding,
Leave you
    without guilt,
Criticize you
    without blaming,
And help you
    without insulting.
If I can have the same
    from you,
Then we can meet and
    enrich each other. [11]

EXERCISE 8: AN INTIMACY CHECKLIST ___

Instructions: The following exercise defines 10 areas of intimacy which are available to persons exploring an intimate marriage.

Not every area of intimacy is equally attractive to every couple. And different stages of marriage will focus more fully on several of these—for example parenting has one character in early marriage, another in middle or later marriage.

Each partner should make an independent rating of the degree of satisfaction with each of these, then the two of you may compare ratings. Look for agreement and disagreement in the degree of fulfillment. Then note which areas are not developed, which carry most of the energy in maintaining closeness.

1. Who is satisfied with an item—how and why?
2. Who is asking for change—what and how?
3. Where is the growing edge in intimacy?
4. What do you want from each other now?

MARITAL INTIMACY CHECKUP

Instructions: Discuss each item until each has expressed at least one strength and one weakness in that area. Then each circle the appropriate level of satisfaction felt. 1 means little, 2 some, 3 average, 4 very good, 5 excellent.

His Rating   *Her Rating*
1. *EMOTIONAL INTIMACY*

1 2 3 4 5   We are able to share a   1 2 3 4 5
wide range of both posi-
tive and negative feelings
without fear of judgment
or rejection.

2. *PHYSICAL INTIMACY*

1 2 3 4 5   We delight in being sen-   1 2 3 4 5
sual, playful and sensitive
in sexual intimacy that is
joyful and fulfilling to us
both.

3. INTELLECTUAL INTIMACY

1 2 3 4 5   We can share ideas, talk   1 2 3 4 5
about issues, debate opin-
ions and notions in
respect for each other's
thoughts.

4. AESTHETIC INTIMACY

1 2 3 4 5   Our delight in beauty—   1 2 3 4 5
music, art, nature, travel,
food, spices, and the
like—is increased by
sharing in the other's
enjoyment of the experi-
ence.

5. PLAY INTIMACY

1 2 3 4 5   We play in a variety of   1 2 3 4 5
ways—sexual, recrea-
tional, relaxing,
competitive—humorous
fun for its own sake.

6. WORK INTIMACY

1 2 3 4 5   We are able to share a   1 2 3 4 5
broad range of tasks in
keeping a home, earning
our living and serving the
church and the commu-
nity.

7. CONFLICT INTIMACY

1 2 3 4 5 We are able to work
through differences
openly and celebrate a
mutually satisfactory solu-
tion.   1 2 3 4 5

8. SPIRITUAL INTIMACY

1 2 3 4 5 We have discovered that
God's grace frees us to
love, to discern what is
right and good and to
honor and celebrate what
is sacred.   1 2 3 4 5

9. PARENTING INTIMACY

1 2 3 4 5 We have found parenting
a shared experience of
being creative, support-
ive, directive, and of freeing the child to grow and
become.   1 2 3 4 5

10. CRISIS INTIMACY

1 2 3 4 5 We are able to stand
together in times of crisis
both external and internal
to the marriage and offer
support and understand-
ing.   1 2 3 4 5

Compare ratings. Discuss differences. Share feelings.
Explore needs. Risk change. Plan growth.

Instructions: Honesty and trust are interdependent elements in intimate relationships. Any increase in one element invites an increase in the other. Any loss in one reduces the other.

1. Read the first set of paragraphs, one from each column to your partner. Then debrief how it illuminates your experience, your feelings, your way of expressing honesty and trust.

2. The other partner replies with his or her understandings of honesty and trust, reflecting on the same two paragraphs.

3. Now the second partner leads off with the next set of paragraphs so that the two, alternately, continue throughout the whole exercise.

4. Do not hesitate to express and explore all disagreements or different ways of expressing your values. Honesty is risking; risking invites trust.

Honesty

I will share myself with you as the person I truly am, without expecting your judgment or fearing your rejection.

I will express myself fully and hear you out completely until our feelings are open and clear.

I will choose my own values, as my center is mine to treasure. I will set my own limits, as my boundaries are mine to keep. I am in charge of myself and therefore responsible.

I will ask for what I want. You are free to say, "Yes, no or later." I will feel anger or withdraw at times. I need to deal with or take care of myself. If I am angry, I will show it openly. I will work through it honestly and fully.

I will know and let you know what I can be and do in our relationship. I will do what I

Trust

I will trust you to listen and hear whether you agree or are upset. I will risk being spontaneous, believing there is room for mistakes.

I will trust you to tell it like it is, so I will not need to mind read or second-guess. I want to hear you fully, see you clearly.

I trust you to protect your core, to maintain your central commitments. I will respect your desires to set limits, to establish your boundaries. You are in charge of your life and fully responsible for yourself.

I trust you to ask for your needs. I will respect your yes, no or later. I can be angry or distant at times since I know you will take care of yourself. If I yell or retreat, I can feel safe, knowing you will hear, not attack or flee.

I trust you to let me know what you want to be or do in relationship. I will not seek to choose to do because I want to do it, not solely because you want me to. Then I will not resent you.

I will not seek to change you, to control or shape your feelings.

I will give you all I can, although sometimes I can give more and at other times I have less.

I do not intend to hurt you although I know hurts will happen. I do want to grow through our disagreements and will accept, not reject our differences.

I am committed to our love. I will always be there for you.

influence what you choose nor control the shape of our relationship. I want you to be free in your choices. Then there need be no resentment.

I trust you to respect and honor me and to deal with your own thoughts and feelings.

I will trust you to give me what you can without expecting you to give more than you are able to give at this moment.

I will trust your good intentions in conflict. If you do something that hurts me, I will believe it has some other reason than the wish to get me or get even with me.

I trust your commitment in love. I will celebrate our meeting.

7
MEANING

MEANING:

HOPES

Hopes shaped by
The Dream are
largely false
hopes which must
eventually die
before real hope
can be born

HOPELESSNESS

Hopes fade,
hopes falter and
fail us; we feel
helpless,
hopeless, empty,
alone.

HOPEFULNESS

Hope rises, as we
find that beneath
the dying hopes
there is hope
which renews and
redirects life.

HOPE

True hope has
emerged and
pushes us on by
healing the past
and pulls us
forward with the
promise of the
future.

TOTAL LOVE

I will love you
utterly, totally,
selflessly.

MIXED LOVE

I will love you as
I can. I need to
know if I am
loved.

REALISTIC LOVE

I will love you as
I love myself.

EQUAL REGARD

I will love you as
I want to be
loved.

HE	BOTH	SHE
But I had my doubts (I kept them to myself). I wondered if she would love me if she knew what I'm really like?	We were so happy together, so full of confidence that everything would work out because we love each other.	
	We smiled a lot, we kept our fears hidden in the hope that they wouldn't happen, but they did.	Do you know what it's like for hope to drain away? When all the reasons you are together look empty?
	It was at the point where it felt like everything was over, like we had nothing left, like something happened.	
I don't know what it was, but there was a turning point.		
	We looked at each other and saw that we still cared.	And we recovered hope, not the old hopes, but hope.

Hope is the energy which sustains a marriage.

Hope is the enemy which destroys a marriage.

Both are true. Hope is both essential energy and enigmatic enemy. Hope sustains the dreams, aims and games that keep couples waiting, pursuing, seducing, manipulating, controlling and being controlled. The hope that these strategies will somehow, someday, in some way pay off holds people back from risking change and living in new and freeing ways. So hope is our worst enemy.

But hope is also the excitement, the lure toward change and growth. When the hope of rediscovering our reason for being together, our resources for loving each other reappears, we can begin all over again.

False Hopes—True Hope

The hopes I hold for my wife or husband can free or bind the relationship. If I love my hopes of what she or he might be or become more than I love the person I have married, the hopes betray us both.

Caring is letting go of hopes so that hope may begin.

Growing is letting hopes die so that hope may be born.

Becoming is letting old hopes pass so hope may appear.

Most marital pain is caused by holding on to past hopes or holding back from the future because of false hopes. So the hopes that have failed us block the healing power of authentic hope.

Hopes must die before authentic hope is born. Just as personal growth proceeds at the pace of our identifying, owning and canceling old self-defeating hopes, so relational growth occurs as we recognize how we are frozen in immature hopes. Then life-giving hope can emerge.

HOPE

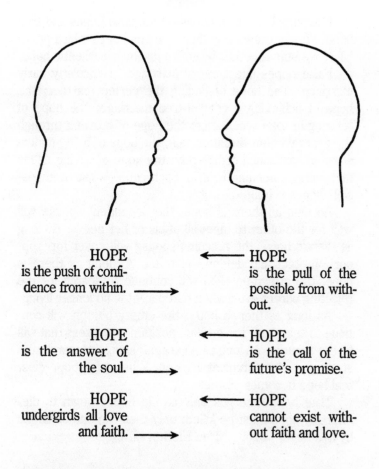

HOPE is the push of confidence from within.	HOPE is the pull of the possible from without.
HOPE is the answer of the soul.	HOPE is the call of the future's promise.
HOPE undergirds all love and faith.	HOPE cannot exist without faith and love.

HOPE MUST BE RENEWED, REDISCOVERED, REBORN AGAIN AND AGAIN IN EVERY LOVING RELATIONSIHP

Figure 1

Marriage is built on hopes—both false hopes and true hope. We are drawn together by many hopes which prove false; we stay together when we discover authentic hope.

False hopes infect every marriage, particularly early marriage. The hope of finding the perfect partner; the hope of achieving a conflict-free marriage; the hope of relaxing in total acceptance; the hope of growing through the years without threat or pain; the hope of being understood instantly and completely; the hope of having needs met without needing to ask. Each couple's list of impossible hopes is long.

As long as there is hope, the dependent spouse will wait for the other to meet all of his or her needs. As long as there's hope, the rescuing spouse will cover for, support, protect and defend the other. As long as there is hope, the grown-up child will continue to search for the rejecting parent even when that parent is no longer living.

As long as there's hope, the empty person will continue to search for the person, position or success that will fill the vacuum. As long as hope continues, the search, the strategies, the pursuit will go on. When such hope dies, real hope becomes possible.

True hope emerges only as old hopes begin to die, "Earthly hope must be killed; only then can one be saved by live hope," wrote Sören Kierkegaard.

The Hope of Perfection

"This could have been a perfect marriage, if it hadn't been for you," says one partner to another in a popular cartoon.

The hopes of finding a perfect partner, a flawless marriage and an endless romance are common in most new love. Once such perfection was the romantic ideal held up for all to emulate. Charlotte Bronte describes such a relationship in *Jane Eyre*:

> I have now been married ten years.
> I know what it is to live entirely
> For and with what I love best on earth . . .
> I know no weariness of my Edward's
> society; he knows none of mine . . .
> We talk, I believe, all day long:
> to talk to each other is but a more
> animated and an audible thinking . . .
> We are precisely suited in character—
> perfect concord is the result.[1]

The perfectionist-type hopes that created this idealized image are: the hope of finding "the one" for me, a dream for me, a peace and calm for me, a security and safety for me, a new justice for me, perhaps a new parent for me, and a loving relationship of unending perfection for me. All this was usually expressed in unselfish words describing a hope, a dream, a peace, a justice, a security for the lover not for the self. What could describe the altruistic, romantic hopes of courtship more concisely? We hope for the other person total happiness in the hope that it will guarantee our own.

A century and a half after Bronte, the process of idealization continues, but the content has changed a number of times as dreams come and go, hopes rise and wane.

The human potentials movement of the last 20 years has raised our hopes of achieving a marital heaven. Such hopes have lured people into marriage for centuries. The heaven promised by romanticism was created of all kinds of projections which invested the other person with all kinds of wonderful characteristics.

Today the hope is in getting our sensitivity, communication and relational process just right. Perhaps if we get in touch with our deepest inner feelings or reclaim all parts of ourselves or get to know all of the other, we can reach heaven. But heavenly marriages are not found here on earth. We each want heaven; we're not satisfied with earth, but that's where we are, that's how it is.

Authentic hope recognizes that we will be both satisfied and dissatisfied with our marriages, that we will be fulfilled and unfulfilled even in our most intimate relationships. Yet we can build a balanced and mature marriage that accepts the ambiguities and imperfections of being human together.

Hope changes and matures throughout marriage. Four distinct patterns emerge which are parallel to the four marriages within a marriage we have been exploring.

Hopes

Marriage one: We are captivated by hopes.

"When I married you, I knew you were right for me, I was absolutely certain that I would never ask if you were the right person for me, I'd never wish to be single again. But I did."

The hopes we bring to marriage and the hopes that bring us to marriage are shaped by (1) our development, (2) our dreams, (3) our depths.

Our hopes extend the unfinished tasks of our developmental journey to that point. So we hope for what was missing, what was needed that went unfulfilled—this lack emerges in deep longings that shape our early marriage.

"This person will fulfill all my dreams of loving and being loved. What was missing in my mother (father) will be completed at last."

"We will create a family where I can begin again, where I can find the justice, the fairness, the acceptance I didn't get from my family."

"This will be a friendship that is so different from my parents, they were always caught in the strangest conflicts that went on and on. That won't happen to us."

"This is the person who is so much like what I want to become. If we are together, I'll be able to find who I really am."

Our hopes express our depths—our unrecognized and truly unknown inner yearnings.

"I think, looking back, I was looking for someone who would give me permission to let go, to be what I was so afraid of being, yet knew I had to become."

We bring these deep levels of hopes into early marriage. Complex and confused as they may be, they bring us together, they bond us to each other. Later we will discover the courage to claim our imperfection, the bravery to embrace our fallibility, the grace to be human. But before that is possible, the hopes must die.

Hopelessness

Marriage two: We are betrayed by our hopes.

"It was like marital burnout. Everything I had hoped would be possible between us had gone up in smoke. What do you do when your marriage is in ashes?"

It is painful when hopes begin to fade. As our dreams falter, we wonder, What is left in our marriage? Perhaps it will not survive? What if we split up? Can we pull it back together?

It is like a death. As dreams die, a part of our ideal self is dying too. She will never be what I wanted with all my heart. He is not able to give what I expected, what I need if we are to be happy. It is a time of despair.

It is a private tragedy, as most couples experience it. It is embarrassing to share with others. They all seem to be succeeding, we are ashamed to admit that our marriage is suffering.

The sense of shame which many couples carry as they go for help for the first time encapsulates them like two lonely astronauts in space suits. As their hopes are dashed, they withdraw in self-protection and self-concealment.

The discovery that this marriage, for all the hopelessness of its feelings, offers us the promise of growth, begins an emotional spring thaw. The winter of discouragement passes and hopefulness begins.

Hopefulness

Marriage three: We are stirred by signs of hope.

"When it seemed like everything was over between us, and there was nothing left but anger, we discovered that our anger still connected us. We still cared much more than we were willing to admit or we wouldn't be so upset."

A new kind of hope stirs within us. The hope which was outer-directed has failed us. The waiting in hope for the dream to come has lost its power. Now hope appears from within. No longer is hope an external magnet; it becomes an internal trusting, believing, willing that presses forward from a confident center. The center may seem small, the confidence weak, yet the voice of hope is insistent.

We become hopeful, we risk hoping. We no longer speak of hope as a picture of coming events, as a compos-

A real
marriage
can begin
at just
the point
where the marriage
appears to be finished.[2]

The adventure
of marriage
is discovering
who the partner
really is.
The excitement
of marriage
is in finding out
who the partner
will become.

ite of collected wishes; we recognize hoping as an active
process of trusting and risking in loving relationship.

The recovery of hope is contagious. As hope returns
to one partner, it spreads to the other through the quiet
language of the heart. One partner may be filled with
hopes that only drive the other away. But when hope
emerges, we touch each other.

Hope

Marriage four: We are set free by Hope.

"There was a time when I thought we could never
part, but I was wrong. Then came the years when I
doubted that we could stay together, but we did. Somewhere along the way, we discovered a new reason for
being together. Call it love, call it faith in each other. I call
it hope."

Hope is the basic ingredient of all marital strength. It is
the uniting, exciting, energizing force that moves us to
risk covenants, to pledge commitments, and to carry out
these promises with fidelity.

Hope provides the basic strength to make love possible. Loving relationship is not a unilateral affection of one
person for an "object" who may or may not love respon-
sively. Loving in marriage is a mutual, reciprocal interchange of affection and loyalty. And this is grounded in
hope, the hope that you will be there when needed, the
hope that you will care in a way that invites us both to
grow, the hope that you will return the love I offer you in a
way that is consistent with yourself.

Hope provides the basic strength which makes fidelity
creative and enduring. Fidelity is the essential basis of
marriage, not love as is popularly assumed.

Emil Brunner the great Swiss theologian has stated this in a terse prioritizing of values:

> Where marriage is based on love, all is lost from the beginning. To build marriage on love is to build on the sand. Marriage is based first on fidelity and second on love.[3]

Perhaps a better way of expressing these two realities is to recognize that both are equally true. As two halves of the truth, they may be seen as polarities which are to be equally prized, balanced, integrated. At a deeper level, love and fidelity may be understood as paradoxical.

Fidelity is an unquestioning commitment to be there for the other. Love is a willingness to see the other in equal regard. The first can be commended; the second, at its most profound level, cannot. The first can be carried out in loyal behavior, the second requires a response, not only in action, but in emotion and the mystery of the spirit. Each is dependent on the other for its fullest expression. I am not creatively faithful to my partner, unless I act in love; I am not authentically loving, except as I live in creative fidelity. No matter how confident I am of your love in this moment, I need to know that you will love tomorrow.

Elizabeth Achtemeier offers a covenant, expressing this tenacious hope that inspires faithful loving (see next page).

Covenant: Where Love and Fidelity Meet in Hope

"The choice of a marital partner is the most decisive choice in life," James Framo has concluded.[5]

In choosing a partner, we choose both who we are to be with and, to a significant degree, who we are to be and become in the following years.

In choosing a partner, we contract to function at a par-

A COVENANT OF HOPE, FAITH AND LOVE

I will be with you
no matter what happens
to us and between us.
If you should become blind tomorrow,
I will be there.
If you achieve no success
and attain no status in our society,
I will be there.

When we argue and are angry,
as we inevitably will,
I will work to bring us together.
When we seem totally at odds
and neither of us is having needs fulfilled,
I will persist in trying to understand
and in trying to restore our relationship.

When our marriage seems utterly sterile
and going nowhere at all,
I will believe that it can work,
and I will want it to work,
and I will do my part to make it work.

And when all is wonderful
and we are happy,
I will rejoice over our life together,
and continue to strive
to keep our relationship growing and strong.[4]

ticular level of maturity, to communicate in given styles of exchange, to relate in certain degrees of closeness and in intimacy.

In risking a covenant with another, one becomes vulnerable to failure as well as given the possibility of success for the first and most crucial time. There are five possibilities: (1) One may overcommit and give up self in dependency on another; (2) one may undercommit and fail to enter the relationship fully; (3) one may miscommit and establish a relationship at too low a level or too conflicted in style; (4) one may fail one's commitment by emotional, spiritual or sexual unfaithfulness; (5) or one may create a mutually satisfying covenant which will support and stimulate maturation throughout a series of stages of growth in marriage.

A marriage is as strong as its covenant is clear. Covenanting is central to personhood. We begin life with implicit covenants—parents will be parents and children can be children. Then covenants take more concrete form—school, peers, work and finally marriage. But the covenant we make in marrying each other needs maturing and revising to match the new movements that happen deep within us and between us. The covenant itself is a pledge that we will each be there for each other in the way that is appropriate to each stage of our maturing, both as individuals and as partners.

Hope unites our love for and faithfulness to the loved person in the pledge with longevity we call covenant. In making a vow, a troth, a covenant, we are making a promise that has permanence, duration, a future as well as a present. Ross Bender writes:

> "The essence of the marriage relationship is to
> be found in covenant, a covenant that is both

similar to and in some respects participates in
the covenant between Christ and his church. In
terms of its practical expression, the key elements in both covenants are love and faithfulness.

A covenant relationship is firm, final and
permanent; it cannot be terminated, only violated. Violating it rips and tears apart that unity
of life which has been sealed by God.[6]

In covenanting, we are pledging our faithfulness
throughout, not just one marriage, but through the unfolding of each marriage within our marriage. Brian Grant
writes of the long-term trajectory of marriage.

An intimate relationship with the same person
over a long period of time—if that relationship
is gratifying—is a revelation to us about the
nature of the world and our own nature. It tells
us, in a way that can't be doubted or disputed,
that with the help of God and this other, we can
establish a satisfying world and life. It tells us
we can have companionship, challenge, conversation, sex and fun. It tells us we can obtain
help from another person when we need it. We
are changed by knowing these things—self-
esteem soars, fear shrinks, hope becomes natural and expectable. The goodness of creation
feels like a reality, and gratitude is a spontaneous offering in return . . . When people live in
this situation, their need to protect themselves
diminishes, leaving energy free for self-
exploration, creativity, the attempt to express

the self, and commitment to the core reality of
other persons and of God.[7]

Hope, Faith, Love

Hope—the trust in each other and God who brings us
together, faith—the faithfulness to work through our life
tasks before God, and love—the willingness to see
another with equal regard—are the basic virtues of the
intimate marriage.

Faith opens our relationship to an accountability to
each other, to God, and to the faith community that gives a
face to the grace of God. In faith, we are not alone in any
of our choices or covenants, we make them before God
and within the context of God's people. When the covenant is being tested as we struggle through the marriage
transitions, the support of communities becomes
extremely important.

There are times when covenants are made between
persons who are toxic or destructive to each other. Violating such a covenant may be a lesser evil than the continuing violation of either person. The severing of covenant is
not good, but it may be the best that we are able to see,
the best we can choose at that point in life.

Such decisions are much too complex, too painful, too
important to be made alone, as they most frequently are.
We need profound support and sensitive guidance. A network of friends in the faith community can offer care during times of separation and divorce. Or it can withdraw,
exclude and condemn those who are severing a covenant,
in the mistaken belief that punitive actions toward them
will protect themselves from their own fear and possible
failure of covenant. Faith and the faith community can help

Be patient toward all
that is unsolved in your heart.
Try to love the questions themselves
like locked rooms
and like books written
in a very foreign tongue.
Do not seek the answers,
which cannot be given you
because you would not
be able to live them.
And the point is
to live everything.
Live the questions now.
Perhaps you will gradually,
without noticing it
live along
some distant day
into the answer.[8]

us be faithful through the rediscovery of hope together or through lives that journey in different directions.

Love as equal regard frees us to prize self and the other partner equally in recreating our relationship or in continuing to value the other person as a person, if the relationship of marriage should end.

Hope is the pull of the possible, the call of the future and its promise. Hope is the push of the confidence within that never lets go of the possibilities.

Marriage, made in faith, celebrated in love and nourished by hope can review itself again and again. It can be recreated, renegotiated and recovenanted in each stage of the life journey. And as we reach toward maturity, we recognize that not everything can be resolved, not all can be answered, not all will be fulfilled in any human relationship, especially marriage. Yet we go on being a part of the imperfect solution, the incomplete answer.

Nothing that we plan in our life together is ever certain, so we live in hope.

Nothing that we risk in our life together is free from the possibility of failure, so we live in faith.

Nothing that we do in our life together is without the danger of hurt and the necessity of healing, so we live in the final form of love which is forgiveness.

EXERCISE 10: COVENANTING OUR HOPE, FAITH, AND LOVE _____

Instructions: To reexamine and reaffirm the covenant which connects your lives, turn back to the Covenant of Hope, Faith and Love by Elizabeth Achtemeier earlier in this chapter.

1. Each person reads the covenant silently; then reflect

on reservations felt, agreements experienced, differences you want to express.

2. Each person reads the covenant aloud to the other, then silently experience the feelings and thoughts which follow.

3. Now take turns debriefing what you have experienced, noting carefully:

   a. this is not a covenant which either "should" adopt, "must" accept, "ought" to hold in perfect agreement.

   b. this is a statement of one ideal for relationship which you try on, like a new hat or hairstyle to see how it fits you;

   c. this is an appropriate model for loving, hoping, trusting, but it is not your model. Write your own and share them together.

NOTES

Chapter 1
1. D. H. Lawrence, *We Need One Another* (New York: Haskell House, Publishers, 1974, p. 37.
2. John R. Neill and David P. Kniskern, eds., *From Psyche to System: The Evolving Therapy of Carl Whitaker* (New York: Guilford Press, 1982), p. 366.
3. Willa Cather. Source unknown.
4. Murray Bowen, *Family Therapy in Clinical Practice* (New York: Aaronson, Jason, Inc., 1978), p. 467ff.
5. James Framo, *Explorations in Marital and Family Therapy* (New York: Springer Publishing Company, 1982), p. 125.
6. Sidney Jourard, *The Transparent Self* (New York: Van Nostrand Reinhold Co., Inc., 1971), p. 108.
7. Diana S. Richmond Garland and David E. Garland, *Beyond Companionship—Christians in Marriage* (Philadelphia: Westminster Press, 1986), p. 10-11.

Chapter 2
1. John R. Neill and David P. Kniskern, eds., *From Psyche to System: The Evolving Therapy of Carl Whitaker* (New York: Guilford Press, 1982), p. 45.
2. Maggie Scarf, *Intimate Partners* (New York: Random House, Inc., 1987), pp. 13-14.
3. By the author.
4. Murray Bowen, Family Therapy in Clinical Practice (New York: Aronson, Jason, Inc., 1978), p. 201.
5. Joseph Luft, *Of Human Interaction* (Palo Alto, CA: Natural Press Books, 1969), pp. 13-16.
6. Ibid.
7. James Framo, *Explorations in Marital and Family Therapy* (New York: Springer Publishing Company, 1982), p. 125.

Chapter 3
1. Daniel Levinson, et.al., *The Seasons of a Man's Life* (New York: Alfred A. Knopf, Inc., 1978), pp. 245-46.
2. Ibid., p. 109.
3. Luciano L'Abate et al., *Family Psychology* (Washington, DC: University Press of America, 1983), p. 82.
4. Denis de Rougemont, *Love in the Western World* (New York: Doubleday Pub-

lishing Co., Anchor Press, 1948), p. 452.
5. Ibid.
6. Ibid., pp. 295-304.
7. Adapted from Sara Cirese, *Quest, A Search for Self* (New York: Holt, Rinehart and Winston, Inc., 1977), p. 175.
8. Evelyn Whitehead and James Whitehead, *Marrying Well* (New York: Doubleday Publishing Co., 1981), p. 204.

Chapter 4
1. R. D. Laing, *The Politics of the Family* (New York: Random House, Inc., 1972), p. 79.
2. Ibid., p. 82.
3. Wayne Brockreide, "Arguers as Lovers," *Philosophy and Rhetoric 5* (Winter 1972): 1-11.
4. David Augsburger, *When Caring Is Not Enough* (Ventura, CA: Regal Books, 1983).
5. Ibid., pp. 5-7.
6. Albert Mehrabian, "Communication Without Words," *Psychology Today* (September 1968), p. 53.
7. Charles Brown and Paul Keller, *From Monologue to Dialogue* (Englewood Cliffs, NJ: Prentice Hall, Inc., 1973), p. 203.
8. Reuel Howe, *The Miracle of Dialogue* (New York: Harper & Row, Publishers, Inc., Winston-Seabury Press, 1966), p. 3.
9. Brown and Keller, *From Monologue to Dialogue*, p. 199.
10. Paul Tournier, *To Understand Each Other* (Atlanta: John Knox Press, 1967), p. 29.
11. Reuel Howe, *Herein Is Love* (Valley Forge, PA: Judson Press, 1961), p. 30.
12. David Augsburger, *Caring Enough to Hear and Be Heard* (Ventura, CA: Regal Books, 1981), pp. 91-92. Adapted.

Chapter 5
1. Barbara Lynch, "Couples: How They Develop and Change," Gestalt Institute News, 1982.
2. James Framo, *Explorations in Marital and Family Therapy* (New York: Springer Publishing Co., Inc., 1982), p. 172.
3. Jay Haley, *Strategies of Psychotherapy* (New York: Grune & Stratton, Inc., 1963), p. 124.
4. Rainer Maria Rilke quoted in Anne Morrow Lindbergh, *Gift from the Sea* (New York: Random House, Inc., Pantheon Books, Inc., 1955), p. 98.
5. Anne Morrow Lindbergh, *Gift from the Sea*, p. 104.

Chapter 6
1. Sonia Murch Nevis and Joseph Zinker, "Marriage, the Impossible Relationship," Gestalt Institute *News* 5 (Fall 1985), p. 1.
2. Luciano L'Abate et al., *Family Psychology* (Washington, DC: University Press of America, 1983), p. 116.
3. John R. Neill and David P. Kniskern, eds., *From Psyche to System: The Evolving Therapy of Carl Whitaker* (New York: Guilford Press, 1982), p. 172.

4. Fritz Junkel, *How Character Develops* (New York: Macmillan Publishing Co., Charles Scribner's and Sons, 1946), pp. 66-86.
5. Luciano L'Abate et al., *Family Psychology,* p. 113.
6. Ulrich Schaffer, *Love Reaches Out* (San Francisco: Harper and Row, Publishers, Inc., 1974), p. 51. Used by permission.
7. Sonia Murch Nevis and Joseph Zinker, "Marriage, the Impossible Relationship, p. 1.
8. Thomas Oden, *Game Free* (New York: Dell Publishing Co., Inc., 1974), pp. 3-4.
9. Alfred North Whitehead, quoted in George Seldes, *The Great Quotations* Simon and Schuster, Inc., Pocket Books, 1967), p. 829.
10. D. H. Lawrence, *We Need One Another* (New York: Haskell House, Publishers, 1974), p. 37.
11. Virginia Satir, *Making Contact* (Berkeley, CA: Ten Speed Press, Celestial Arts Publishing Co., 1976), p. 19.

Chapter 7
1. Charlotte Bronte, *Jane Eyre* (New York: Dodd, Mead and Co., Inc., 1941), p. 543. Public domain.
2. Sidney Jourard, *The Transparent Self* New York: Van Nostrand Reinhold Co., Inc., 1975), p. 108.
3. Emil Brunner, *The Divine Imperative* (London: Lutterworth Press, 1942), pp. 344-45.
4. Elizabeth Achtemeier, *The Committed Marriage* (Philadelphia: Westminster Press, 1976), p. 41.
5. James Framo, *Explorations in Marital and Family Therapy* (New York: Springer Publishing Company, 1982), p. 126.
6. Ross Bender, *Christians in Families* (Scottdale, PA: Herald Press, 1982), p. 61.
7. Brian Grant, *Reclaiming the Dream* (Nashville: Abingdon Press, 1986), p. 18.
8. Rainer Maria Rilke, *Letters to a Young Poet* (New York: W.W. Norton & Co., Inc., 1963), p. 35.

BIBLIOGRAPHY

Achtemeier, Elizabeth. *The Committed Marriage*. Philadelphia: The Westminster Press, 1976.

Augsburger, David. *Caring Enough to Confront*. Ventura, CA: Regal Books, 1980.

_____. *Caring Enough to Forgive*. Ventura, CA: Regal Books, 1982.

_____. *Caring Enough to Hear and Be Heard*. Ventura, CA: Regal Books, 1981.

_____. *Cherishable: Love and Marriage*. Scottdale, PA: Herald Press, 1970.

_____. *When Caring Is Not Enough*. Ventura, CA: Regal Books, 1983.

_____. *When Enough Is Enough*. Ventura, CA: Regal Books, 1984.

Bender, Ross. *Christians in Families*. Scottdale, PA: Herald Press, 1982.

Bly, Robert. *Loving a Woman in Two Worlds*. Garden City, NY: Doubleday and Company, 1985.

Brockriede, Wayne. "Arguers as Lovers." *Philosophy and Rhetoric* 5 (Winter 1972):1-11.

Bronte, Charlotte. *Jane Eyre*. New York: Dodd, Mead and Co., Inc., 1941.

Brown, Charles T. and Keller, Paul W. *From Monologue to Dialogue*. Englewood Cliffs: Prentice Hall, 1973.

Brunner, Emil. *The Divine Imperative*. London: Lutterworth Press, 1942.

Carter, Elizabeth and McGoldrick, Monica. *The Family Life Cycle*. New York: Gardner Press Inc., 1980.

Cirese, Sara. *Quest, A Search for Self*. New York: Holt, Rinehart and Winston, Inc., 1977.

de Rougemont, Denis. *Love in the Western World*. New York: Doubleday Author Books, 1956.

Faul, John and Augsburger, David. *Beyond Assertiveness*. Waco, TX: Word Books, 1978.

Framo, James. *Explorations in Marital and Family Therapy*. New York: Springer Publishing Co. Inc., 1982.

Grant, Brian. *Reclaiming the Dream*. Nashville: Abingdon Press, 1986.

Haley, Jay. *Strategies of Psychotherapy*. New York: Grune and Stratton Inc., 1963.

Howe, Reuel. *Herein Is Love*. Valley Forge: Judson Press, 1961.

_____. *The Miracle of Dialogue*. New York: Winston-Seabury Press, 1966.

L'Abate, Luciano. *Family Psychology*. Washington, D.C.: University Press of
America, 1983.

Laing, R.R. *The Politics of the Family*. New York; Random House Inc., 1972.

Levinson, Daniel J., et al. *The Seasons of a Man's Life*. New York: Alfred A.
Knopf, Inc., 1979.

Lindbergh, Anne Morrow. *Gift from the Sea*. New York: Random House, Inc.,
Pantheon Books, Inc., 1955.

Luft, Joseph. *Of Human Interaction*. Palo Alto, CA: Natural Press Books, 1969.

Lynch, Barbara. "Couples: How They Develop and Change." News. Cleveland:
Gestalt Institute, 1982.

Mehrabian, Albert. "Communication Without Words." *Psychology Today* September 1968:53.

Mood, John. *Rilke on Love and Other Difficulties*. New York: W. W. Norton and
Co., Inc., 1975.

Neill, John R. and Kniskern, David P., eds. *From Psyche to System: The Evolving
Therapy of Carl Whitaker*. New York: Guilford Press, 1982.

Nevis, Sonia Murch and Zinker, Joseph. "Marriage the Impossible Relationship."
News. Cleveland: Gestalt Institute, 5 (Fall 1985): 1.

Rilke, Rainer Maria. *Letters to a Young Poet*. New York: W. W. Norton and Co.,
Inc., 1963.

Satir, Virginia. *Making Contact*. Berkeley, CA: Ten Speed Press, Celestial Arts
Publishing Co., 1976.

Scarf, Maggie. *Intimate Partners*. New York: Random House Inc., 1987.

Schaffer, Ulrich. *Love Reaches Out*. San Francisco: Harper and Row Publishers,
Inc., 1974.

Tolstoy, Leo. *Anna Karenina*. New York: Mead and Co. Inc., 1966.

Tournier, Paul. *To Understand Each Other*. Atlanta: John Knox Press, 1967.

Waugh, Evelyn. *Brideshead Revisited*. Boston: Little, Brown and Co. Inc., 1946.

Whitehead, Evelyn and Whitehead, James. *Marrying Well*. New York: Doubleday and Co., 1981.

RECOVERY OF HOPE
NETWORK

This recovery-of-hope book was written to help couples rebuild hope when relationships feel hopeless. It is also a *Recovery of Hope* book designed as a part of an international program for renewing of hope among troubled couples.

Recovery of Hope is a community program which reaches out to married couples during times of marital stress and despair. These programs can be found throughout Canada and the United States. They offer hope, guidance, support and spiritual nurturance for couples experiencing marital difficulty by bringing them together in a three-hour session where they hear presentations by three couples who have experienced despair and a rebirth in their marriage.

Participating couples are not asked to share their own situation, but often find a spark of hope in hearing the stories of others. Each couple is provided a marriage counselor and given the opportunity to prepare a recovery plan. A caring couple is made available for each participating couple to provide them prayer support throughout their reconciliation time.

The center providing the *Recovery of Hope* program works to provide a total range of needed resources for each couple. Often this includes marital counseling, support and/or therapy groups, as well as educational classes. While almost 80 percent of the couples who come believe they will end up divorced, two out of every three couples opt to make and work on their recovery plan. Some of the couples who have attended *Recovery of Hope* in the past are now sharing their story of hope as a ministry to others. For further information, you may write:

**Recovery of Hope Network
335 North Waco
Wichita, Kansas 67202-1158**

Phone 1-800-327-2590

SUBJECT INDEX

Exercises and Experiences